Georgia's Signers
And The
Declaration Of
Independence

THE SIGNING OF THE DECLARATION OF INDEPENDENCE, BY JOHN TRUMBULL

Mural in the United States Capitol, Washington, D.C.

Georgia's Signers

And The
Declaration
Of
Independence

By

Edwin C. Bridges,
Harvey H. Jackson,
Kenneth H. Thomas, Jr.,
and
James Harvey Young

ATLANTA
CHEROKEE PUBLISHING COMPANY

Copyright © 1981

Cherokee Publishing Company

ISBN: 0-87797-315-6

Georgia's signers and the Declaration of Independence / Edwin C. Bridges ... [et al.]. — Atlanta : Cherokee Pub. Co., 1981.
    106 p., [22] leaves of plates : ill. ; 24 cm.
    Includes bibliographies and index.
    ISBN 0-87797-055-6 : $8.95

    1. United States. Declaration of Independence—Signers—Biography—Addresses, essays, lectures. 2. Legislators—Georgia—Biography—Addresses, essays, lectures. 3. Georgia—History—Revolution, 1775-1783—Biography—Addresses, essays, lectures. I. Bridges, Edwin C.
E221.G43   1981   81-67795
                              973.3'13'0922—dc19
                                          AACR 2   MARC
Library of Congress

PRINTED IN THE UNITED STATES OF AMERICA

Cherokee Publishing Company
P O Box 1730, Marietta, GA 30061

Table of Contents

Illustrations

(For Credits, see page 98.)

Preface

In April 1980, papers on Georgia's signers of the Declaration of Independence — Lyman Hall, Button Gwinnett, and George Walton — were read before the spring meeting of the Georgia Historical Society in Savannah. During the informal discussion that followed it was lamented that most published studies of these "founding fathers" were outdated, inaccurate, or located in scholarly journals not readily available to the general public. This meant that individuals interested in Georgia's signers had to rely on older works that not only perpetuated myths and misinformation but often cast their subjects in such heroic molds that their real accomplishments were either overlooked or obscured. As a result most Georgians, and for that matter most Americans, know little of substance about the careers of Hall, Walton, and Gwinnett — beyond the fact that they signed the Declaration.

In the same discussion it was further noted that the papers just presented not only shed new light on the lives of the signers but also complemented each other in such a way as to give the audience a fresh look at the causes and consequences of the struggle for independence south of the Savannah River. These observations prompted a suggestion that the authors consider combining their essays and publishing them in a single volume. Such a book, it was observed, would fill a long-standing need and would give citizens of the state, as well as others interested in early American history, a lively and informative account of the men and the era in which they lived.

This was not the first time such a plan had been recommended. When the Savannah program was initially announced, Robert S. Davis, Jr., an active researcher and writer in colonial and Revolutionary history, recognized the papers' potential and urged a similar course of action. Mr. Davis also suggested that if publication was being considered, the appeal of the book might be further broadened if Kenneth H. Thomas, Jr., who had done considerable work in the field, could be persuaded to contibute a selection on the genealogy of the signers. Such an addition seemed natural to all concerned, thus, the project assumed its final shape.

It should be noted here at the outset that, despite the obvious way each essay relates to the others, each is the product of individual effort and is marked by its author's own particular point of view. In compiling the book no attempt was made to arrive at a single interpretation of events common to the signers' careers. In fact, the more perceptive reader will note that, although the writers agree on critical facts and dates, they are not entirely one on the importance of what occurred or on the motives of the men involved. That, however, is how it should be, for history is more than agreed-upon facts and dates. History is the account of what men did and why they did it — and the latter, especially where the Georgia signers are concerned, continues open to debate.

The authors do not claim that these essays are the final word on their respective subjects. As long as historians research the field, existing interpretations will be re-evaluated and, at times, overturned. This collection is part of the ongoing process, part of the continuing assessment of the past that makes history more than a "cut and dried" subject for study. These articles are supported by the most thorough research on Hall, Gwinnett, and Walton done to date. They fill gaps in our knowledge, scrape away many of the false assumptions that have long clung to the signers' careers, and assess the forces that made them the men they were. Although specific documentation has not been provided, a detailed "Note on Sources" is included at the end of each essay in order that those wishing to dig deeper into the lives and times of these patriots might do so. It is hoped what is presented here will give readers a new, or renewed, appreciation of Georgia's revolution and her revolutionaries. If that is the result, the authors will feel their efforts amply recompensed.

HARVEY H. JACKSON

Georgia's Signers
And The
Declaration Of
Independence

Chapter I

PRELUDE TO INDEPENDENCE

Edwin C. Bridges

Although the roots of the American Revolution can be traced back to many areas of colonial life, the immediate chain of events that led to a declaration of independence began in December 1773 with the "Boston Tea Party." Furious about the colonists' destruction of property and their disregard for law, George III and Prime Minister Lord North determined that the people of Massachusetts should be punished. In early 1774 Parliament passed a series of measures that Americans called the "intollerable acts." These acts closed the port of Boston, unseated the charter government of Massachusetts, altered court procedures, and provided for the quartering of British soldiers. As the news of Parliament's actions reached America, several colonies simultaneously issued calls for a general congress to consider a united response. Pleased with these expressions of support, the Massachusetts assembly suggested that a meeting be held in Philadelphia that September. The First Continental Congress formally convened in Carpenters' Hall on Monday morning, September 5, 1774. There were 56 delegates in all — the most able leaders of twelve American colonies. The only colony not represented was Georgia.

Having been founded only 41 years before the First Continental Congress, Georgia was the youngest of the thirteen American colonies. For its first twenty years the colony had languished under the well-meaning but restrictive administration of a board of philanthropic trustees. Most Georgians regarded the 1754 inauguration of royal government as a relief and a blessing. Despite a relative lack of success in the first two gubernatorial appointments, the colony found a strong and respected leader in James Wright, who was appointed governor in 1761. Wright energetically supported the material interests of the colony: the growth of agriculture and commerce, defense against Indian attacks, and continued territorial expansion.

Despite this new period of growth fostered by Wright, Georgia in 1774 still consisted of only a small line of settlements along the Atlantic Ocean and the Savannah River. Very few of the colony's approximately 30,000 people lived more than twenty miles inland from these two links of its eastern boundary. Indians were able to appear without warning on the streets of Augusta, and the threat of an attack was a constant concern of the settlers. Because revenues generated by taxes were only a modest £3000, the major portion of the funds required to support the colonial administration and to protect the citizens was provided by Great Britain. This outside financial and military support allowed Governor Wright to exercise stronger control and greater independence than was possible for governors in other colonies, where representative assemblies controlled the purse strings. This dependence on Great Britain naturally fostered among Georgians a reluctance to offend or alienate the source of their support.

While the other colonies responded to the plight of Boston with bold demonstrations of solidarity, Georgians were able to utter only the most timid expressions of concern. In early July 1774 Georgians read in their newspaper that South Carolinians had just met in Charleston to denounce the Intolerable Acts and to select their representatives for the upcoming congress in Philadelphia. A few days afterward, an anonymous handbill was circulated in Savannah calling for a meeting "at the Exchange" to consider "the critical situation to which the British Colonies in America are likely to be reduced." Governor Wright maintained in a letter to the British secretary of state that this outburst was not only inspired by but was directly instigated by "Our Neighbors in Carolina . . . [who] have been very busy in Sending Hand Bills, Letters and Public Invitations, etc., etc., to Stir up the People here. . . ."

The meeting at the Exchange produced few important results. So hesitant were the leading citizens to offend royal officials that the assemblage had difficulty finding someone to take the chair. After completing their deliberations, the protestors concluded that they did not represent the entire province and that a second meeting should be held on August 10 to allow for broader participation. Governor Wright used the interval between these meetings to try to squelch the protests and to prevent the second meeting. The fact that a meeting was held at all is testimony to the resolution and courage of the protest leaders.

The representatives at the August 10 meeting were able to agree only on a relatively mild set of pronouncements — declaring that Americans should have the same rights and responsibilities as "their fellow-subjects in Great Britain" and that the Intolerable Acts were "contrary to our idea of the British Constitution." A letter campaign followed in the Savannah newspaper about whether these pronouncements actually represented the views of most Georgians. The supporters of the royal government professed their willingness to let "the world . . . judge whether the meeting of the tenth inst., held by a few persons in a tavern, with the doors shut, can, with any appearance of truth or decency, be called a general meeting of the inhabitants of Georgia." Even though loyalist critics may have overstated the weakness of Georgia's protest movement, the participants at the August 10 meeting acknowledged their own doubts when they failed to send delegates to the Continental Congress in Philadelphia.

Through the autumn of 1774, while supporters from Georgia to New Hampshire waited anxiously, the delegates in Philadelphia tried to fashion a policy that would satisfy two fundamental interests. They had to show clearly their common cause with the people of Massachusetts, but they also wished to avoid a final break with Great Britain. Congress's address to King George professed the Americans' continued allegiance to His Majesty's person, family, and government and pleaded for a redress of their grievances. At the same time, however, Congress prepared a set of resolutions that came to be called the "Agreements of Association," or simply "the Association." These agreements called for the end to all trade with Great Britain until the actions against Massachusetts were rescinded. Other provisions of the Association sought to strengthen the ability and the will of the people to resist further British coercion — such as a resolution to discourage "every species of extravagance and dissipation, especially all horse-racing, and all kinds of gaming, cock-fighting, exhibitions of shows, plays, and other expensive diversions and entertainments." To enforce these resolutions, the Congress called for local committees to be chosen "in every county, city, and town . . . to observe the conduct of all persons touching this association."

When the terms of the Association were published in Georgia, protest leaders called for another meeting in Savannah to consider adopting the agreements. The January 1775 provincial congress was unable to agree on the resolutions without alterations to modify the adverse impact on Georgia. Apparently these modified agreements were not even published. The representatives did agree to send a slate of delegates from Georgia to the next Continental Congress, but later the delegates themselves decided not to attend. They wrote to the president of the Congress that their support in Georgia was not sufficient for the delegates to "pledge themselves for the execution of any measure whatsoever."

Following this dismal showing, Georgia's voices of protest remained subdued through the winter and into the spring of 1775. It was not until May that a shock wave arrived that finally galvanized the reluctant rebels into concerted action with the other American colonies: the news of the fighting at Lexington and Concord. Immediately, a band of patriots broke into the public magazine and seized the province's powder supply. A few weeks later, protestors spiked the province's cannon to prevent the firing of salutes in celebration of the king's birthday. Now the emboldened protestors gathered openly at Tondee's Tavern, raised their liberty pole, and quaffed their toasts to American liberty.

FLAGS OF REVOLUTIONARY GEORGIA

In June, a public notice signed by Noble W. Jones, Archibald Bulloch, John Houstoun, and George Walton called for the election of delegates to a new provincial assembly to convene in early July. No longer intimidated by Governor Wright, the July provincial congress immediately accepted all the provisions of the Agreements of Association -- without any changes -- and appointed new delegates to the Continental Congress. The congress also began steps to establish an independent government to supplant royal authority in Georgia. By July 8, 1775, Governor Wright admitted to the British secretary of state 'that "the Powers of Government are wrested out of my Hands."

Through the remainder of 1775, the Georgia revolutionaries continued to tighten their grip on the reins of government. In August there was a purge of the militia which allowed only officers who swore their support of the association to continue in command. Other important institutions, such as the churches and the courts, were also cut off from royal control or influence. In January 1776 another provincial congress decided to arrest Governor Wright to prevent him from assisting the British naval vessels cruising along the Georgia coast. Realizing that all was lost, Governor Wright broke his oath and fled to the ships, leaving Georgia in the hands of the victorious revolutionary leaders.

The same congress that ordered Wright's arrest also selected a new slate of delegates to represent Georgia in the Continental Congress. Of the five delegates chosen, three made the trip to Philadelphia: Button Gwinnett, Lyman Hall, and George Walton. During early 1776, the rebel leaders were distracted by several small skirmishes with British naval units that continued to threaten the Georgia coast, and instructions for the delegates were not prepared until April. Aware of Georgia's remote situation, state officials were purposefully broad in their formal instructions, authorizing the delegates "to propose, join, and concur, in all such measures as you shall think calculated for the common good."

Meanwhile, in Philadelphia as in other parts of the continent, a major shift in public opinion was taking place. The desire to avoid a final break with Britain was giving way to the vision of an independent new nation. The Americans had initially denounced the British measures against them as the work of an overweening, aggressive Parliament, but they held onto the hope that the king was merely the temporary victim of bad advice by misguided counselors. They hoped that somehow he would come to realize the justice of their cause. Joseph Reed, a delegate from Pennsylvania, had called it a "strange reluctance in the minds of many to cut the bond which ties us to Great Britain."

By the spring of 1776 this reluctance was beginning to give way. Thomas Paine's *Common Sense* both exemplified and helped accelerate this change of sentiment: "Reconciliation is *now* a fallacious dream. . . . Everything that is right or natural pleads for separation. The blood of the slain, the weeping voice a nature cries, '*tis time to part.* . . ." The issue was hotly argued in all the American colonies, and it lay behind many of the deliberations of the Continental Congress. Through the spring, in one measure after another, the Congress adopted new practices and policies that systematically severed the cords binding America to Great Britain.

All congressional delegates were governed by the formal instructions of the governments they represented, and many of the delegates were strictly limited in the measures they could approve. As public sentiment for independence continued to mount, new delegations and new instructions began to arrive that permitted the delegates to become increasingly defiant of the British. In May 1776 new instructions from Virginia directed the state's delegates to propose a declaration of American independence. On June 7, Richard Henry Lee, in obedience to these instructions, offered a resolution declaring "that these limited Colonies are, and of right ought to be, free and independent States." Lee's motion was seconded by John Adams. Although more cautious delegates succeeded in an agreement to postpone the question until July 1, the Congress appointed a committee of Thomas Jefferson, John Adams, Benjamin Franklin, Roger Sherman, and Robert Livingston to prepare a draft that in turn could be considered on that date.

Button Gwinnett and Lyman Hall were the first two members of the new Georgia delegation to reach Philadelphia. They arrived on May 20, just after Virginia had adopted its resolution for a declaration of independence. The breadth of their instructions and the firmness of their resolve gave great encouragement to advocates of independence such as John Adams. George Walton, the third Georgia delegate, had been slowed on route by illness and by his efforts to recruit troops from North Carolina and Virginia to serve in Georgia. On June 17, Walton wrote from Williamsburg to a colleague in Georgia that he was just about to leave for Philadelphia. He happily reported that he was "not too late for the great American question — if a question now it may be called." Although the records do not indicate the precise time of his arrival, Walton appears to have taken his seat in Congress on July 1, the day scheduled for consideration of "the great question."

After protracted debate, the question of declaring independence was finally put on July 2, and the Congress formally adopted Lee's resolution that the "United Colonies" should from that time forth be free and independent states. A formal decision to claim independence, however, was not sufficient. Reasons had to be given — to unite the American people and to justify their cause to the world. The Congress immediately began consideration of the declaration that Jefferson and his committee had prepared. There were a few changes in the draft — one at the instigation of the South Carolina and Georgia delegates to delete a passage denouncing the slave trade.

On the evening of July 4 the document was finally approved, with twelve states voting in favor and one, New York, remaining silent. Following the adoption of the Declaration of Independence, the Congress resolved that it be printed and distributed as widely as possible so "that the people may be universally informed of it." It was welcomed by joyful celebrations up and down the Atlantic seaboard. With many other weighty matters demanding its attention, the Congress did not order an engrossed copy prepared until July 19. The formal signing of the engrossed copy took place on August 2, with the three Georgia delegates affixing their signatures in the first column on the left side.

Chapter II

FACTIONAL POLITICS IN REVOLUTIONARY GEORGIA

Harvey H. Jackson

T he effort that resulted in the appointment of Georgia's three delegates to the Second Continental Congress — Lyman Hall, Button Gwinnett, and George Walton — was not indicative of a continuing harmony among revolutionary forces within the colony. Georgia politics involved disputes between diverse factions — factions that existed before the signing of the Declaration of Independence and survived after it. At times these factions did arrive at compromises in order to direct their collective efforts against the British, but these were seldom permanent. When the divisive issues became important enough, the consensus disintegrated and the struggle over "who would rule at home" flared once more.

The internal conflict that did so much to shape revolutionary politics in Georgia focused on two elements within the Whig movement: the "radicals", led at the outset by men from St. John's Parish, and the "conservatives", whose leadership came primarily from Savannah and Christ Church Parish. These two groups hardly represented the full scope of Whig opinion , yet as opposition to British policies reached a climax the "movement" began to polarize about these extremes. Risks inherent in promoting factionalism at a time when unity was essential were obvious enough; but the reward, ultimate control of the system being created, made the risk well worth taking.

It was in the Commons House of Assembly, during the legislative-executive conflicts of the late 1760s and early 1770s, that the goals of Georgia's future Whigs, conservative and radical, began to crystallize. Following the example set by its northern counterparts, the lower house attempted to expand its powers over appointments and finances, as well as to serve as a forum for discussing and even denouncing British policies. Initial efforts were all but negated by Governor James Wright, who possessed the independence other colonial governors lacked and was determined to quash any move to expand legislative powers at the expense of executive authority.

At first the lower house acted in good English constitutional fashion and worked to establish precedents in its favor. But that tactic met ever-increasing resistance from the governor, his council, and other supporters, convincing many legislators that reform, if it came, would have to be initiated outside normal channels. Frustrations rising from their inability to circumvent the executive coincided with the tension created by American protests of Britain's "new colonial policy" until, by 1774, it was difficult to tell which royal government disturbed the emerging Whigs more — the one at home or the one across the sea.

In colonial Georgia any reference to Assembly policy referred, obliquely, to the policy of Christ Church, for the influence of that parish permeated the lower house. Men from Savannah and its environs dominated committees, framed laws, defended privileges, and in general defined and directed the struggle with the executive. Of the fifty-two leading assemblymen during the royal period (based upon service on major committees), twenty-six represented Christ Church at least once in their careers. Twenty-seven of the fifty-two leaders had such a greater portion of the committee assignments that they were designated by historian Jack P. Greene as being the "first rank"; and, of those, fourteen were from Christ Church. In contrast, between 1754 and 1776, St. John's Parish had only five assemblymen among the fifty-two leaders, and only one of those was considered to be in the "first rank" — and he for only one year. Although one might expect that as St. John's Parish grew older and more populous its representatives would have been able to erode the power of Christ Church, just the opposite is true. Between 1765 and 1775 Christ Chruch actually tightened its grip on the Assembly's leadership, for of the thirteen members classified as "first rank" during that period eight were from that parish.

This disproportionate and extraordinary influence exercised by the Christ Church faction enabled it to take an early and commanding lead of those who came to be called Whigs. They seemed an unlikly lot to serve as the vanguard of Georgia's revolutionary movement. Many had prospered under royal rule and had close ties with the governor's supporters. Conscious that they were as much a part of the colonial "establishment" as the executive, the Christ Church faction proposed to alter, not overturn, the system: to amend it to resemble that of the mother country where Parliament, rather than the crown, shaped domestic policy; but to make the change with as little accompanying disturbance as possible.

The citizens of St. John's, chiefly descendants of New England Puritans, still retained, according to the governor, "a strong tincture of Republican or Oliverian principles." Like their Christ Church neighbors, they were deeply troubled by Wright's attitude toward legislative expansion and were willing to work to limit executive power. But in reality, St. John's political goals were blocked by a force that seemed equally as imposing as the governor — the Christ Church faction.

St. John's leadership belonged to the same provincial elite that filled the Commons House, but they had not been able to translate that status into political power. Though the lower house was the obvious place for men of republican sentiments to seek an outlet for political amibitions, in the Georgia legislature Christ Church led and St. John's was relegated to a secondary position. The governor's authority was certainly a matter of concern, but to minimize his role would have only partially solved St. John's problem. The power of Christ Church had to be reduced as well.

As Georgia politics was evolving it might have been decades before representatives from St. John's occupied positions in the "first rank" of the colonial government; but they did not have to wait for evolution. The growing dissatisfaction with British policies provided an excellent vehicle for attacking not only the royal government but also a means of challenging the whole colonial power structure — and from outside the Christ Church-controlled Assembly. In this way the old order could be brought down and a new one, with St. John's a prominent member, raised in its place. How active St. John's had been in earlier anti-British protests is difficult to determine; however, in the summer of 1774, that parish served notice of its intent to influence and even dominate the Whig movement.

On August 10, at a meeting called in Savannah to protest the Intolerable Acts, St. John's made her initial bid for power and failed. After the unanimous passage of eight resolutions defending American rights and denouncing the acts, radicals proposed what seemed to be the next logical step — that delegates be sent to the Continental Congress. Conservative opposition was immediate.

To send representatives to an unsanctioned congress meant going outside the system, creating new mechanisms of government that could threaten the old. Conservatives were in no mood to unleash forces they might be unable to control. Their ranks closed and held firm: The resolution failed.

After the meeting adjourned the radicals attempted to shift the center of Whig activity from Savannah to Midway, in St. John's Parish. There, in friendlier surroundings, they planned to gain control of the movement. The call went out for other parishes to send delegates to join them, but most Georgians, as yet uncommitted to the Whig cause, felt no desire to interject themselves into what seemed only another phase in the longstanding struggle between Christ Church and St. John's. The radicals, unable to convince the people that they championed any cause but their own, found only three parishes willing to support their efforts. With that the advantage shifted back to Christ Church.

Conservatives moved quickly to capitalize on the radicals' failure. Recognizing the need for more positive actions in the light of radical precedents, they called for a provincial congress to meet in Savannah. But it was not as "revolutionary" a move as it might seem. Though it was an *extra-legal* congress, the delegates would meet in the conservatives' stronghold and under the watchful eye of the Christ Church-dominated Assembly — hardly a situation to threaten the *status quo*.

Realizing the movement had to be kept alive if any changes were to come, radical leaders endorsed the congress but not the conservatives' "wait and see" policy. Instead they urged other parishes to follow their example and adopt the Continental Association before the congress convened. Thus, if the conservatives planned to use the meeting to delay such action they would be presented with a *fait accompli.*

The call for Georgians to rally to the conservative standard drew a slightly better response than did radical efforts; but most parishes still saw little to gain in taking sides in an old conflict, even if it was furbished with new issues and rhetoric. St. John's in spite of her endorsement, also refused to attend, for if this congress succeeded where the Midway meetings had failed, conservative claims to Whig leadership would have been difficult to dispute. If support for the "common cause" meant perpetuation of Christ Church domination, then St. John's would have none of it. They were willing to let the provincial congress serve as a precedent for organized protest outside the system but not as a vehicle for conservative policy.

But circumstances were forcing conservatives to alter their course of moderation. The standard of "Whiggishness" set by the radicals had to at least be acknowledged, or loyalty to the "cause" might be questioned. It was a problem of how to attack the system without threatening it, and their solution revealed the mixture of political sophistication and naivete that ultimately became the hallmark of conservative strategy. The congress adopted the Continental Association, with reservations, and selected gentlemen from Christ Church to go to Philadelphia. Realizing it spoke for only a small segment of the colony, though, it called on the Assembly to approve its actions. Superficially the latter seemed an excellent tactic, for the Assembly's approval would lend legitimacy to the congress, and, considering the conservatives' influence, that body could be expected to ratify without radicalizing. Before the Assembly could act, however,

Governor Wright prorogued it.

It is difficult to imagine that Wright was expected to do otherwise, but even so the governor's action had a profound effect on many conservatives. The line was drawn, limitations on protest within the system defined. It was clear that no reforms were possible so long as the executive controlled the means of reformation. In order to break the governor's power and expand their own, conservatives would have to carry their protests far outside normal channels. It was there, outside the restrictions and security of the established order, that the radicals waited — ready to make changes of their own.

Rather than protesting a predictable proroguing by a royal governor who was only part of their problem, the radicals moved to establish their credentials solidly as supporters of American liberty so that conservatives would appear irresolute in comparison. To a degree they succeeded. Though some of their efforts may have produced more symbolism than substance, when Lyman Hall was sent to Philadelphia as their personal delegate, St. John's and the radicals showed a willingness to act that could not be ignored. Christ Church had to follow or be left behind.

Conservatives were under pressure from other quarters as well, for Wright's action did what previous radical and conservative efforts had failed to do: It created a colony-wide Whig movement. Outraged by the proroguing, many un-committed Georgians now joined the "cause". In Savannah Whigs of all classes vented their frustrations through some of the most extreme protests Georgians had witnessed. News of fighting in the north pumped additional adrenalin into the already hyper-tense situation, and, as the protests spread to other parishes, Wright's ability to govern decreased with alarming rapidity. The Assembly, called to meet in May, failed to raise a quorum; and when this was followed, on July 4, 1775, by the meeting of a second provincial congress made up of delegates from all but the two most remote parishes, it became clear that royal government was on the verge of collapse. The Whigs were at last ready and able to assume authority.

The second provincial congress did more than accentuate Wright's inability to govern; it marked the formation of Georgia's first revolutionary consensus. At some point during the meetings and political maneuvering of that spring the Whigs — radical, conservative, and moderate — had agreed to unite their efforts in the common cause. But it was a consensus on what was to be destroyed, not on what was to be created. All elements agreed that the executive's authority had to be minimized, but beyond that immediate goal the divisions ran as deeply as before. (It is difficult to determine if, this early in the struggle, any radicals had concluded that separation from Britain was necessary for their aims to be realized; but it is clear that many conservatives still felt it possible to achieve their goals within the empire, and they were prepared to use the provincial congress to those ends.)

Though on the surface compromise and continuity seemed the themes of the congress, in reality conservatives dominated its committees and shaped most of its policies. Apparently such was the condition for their participation. But the radicals had not given without gaining. The "revolution" and their political hopes were kept alive, while the conservatives policy of moderation had been abandoned. Equally important, it was decided that at future meetings representation would be on a more equitable basis and, either in an effort to win the people to their side or as a reward for their aid, suffrage would be granted upon payment of the general tax. Both reforms were ultimately to work to the radicals' advantage. Thus Georgians were taking positive steps to change the system that governed them, and if the system could be changed, the radicals surely reasoned, so could its leadership.

Its work done, the provincial congress adjourned, leaving parish and parochial committees to carry out its directives. In the flurry of activity that followed, it was difficult to tell radical from conservative, so intent were both on proving their ability and dedication. But as the Whigs set about dismantling royal government, what had been essentially an upper-class movement began to change. The "common folk" — urban mechanics and artisans, small farmers, back-country people, and the like — had played an active but ill-defined role in the protests since the beginning; but as each faction sought popular approval for its actions the importance of the "people" grew. Now, with the lowering of suffrage requirements, they became the key element in the struggle for control of Georgia's revolution.

The radicals soon embarked on a strategy designed to bring the various "popular" groups into their camp, but it was not a simple task. Radical leaders had little in common with the "masses", and they, in turn, felt a natural skepticism toward any "aristocrat" who claimed to speak for their interests. However, there was one point of agreement, and that proved enough. All saw the conservatives as perpetuators of the system from which they had been excluded. Breaking the power of the governor had been the goal of the radical-conservative coalition; breaking the power of the conservatives was to be the goal of the "Popular Party".

But the Popular Party was not created overnight, and, while it was being formed, the radicals found it necessary to maintain their alliance of convenience with the conservatives. Even though royal government had been rendered ineffective, much of its machinery still remained, and a mass defection of conservatives could easily revive it. Aware of that situation, the radicals moved with caution. A few conservatives were disturbed enough by the republican drift of the movement to abandon the cause, but most felt it folly to surrender authority just when success seemed so near. Still feeling a solution was possible within the empire, conservatives were sustained by the belief that they would ultimately create a new Georgia in their own image.

For the radicals it was a trying time. In January of 1776 they were able to elect one of their leaders, Button Gwinnett, as colonel of the newly-created Georgia continental battalion only to be forced, under conservative and moderate pressure, to surrender that powerful post. To compensate for their loss, Gwinnett was appointed to join his friend Lyman Hall in Philadelphia. Thus the radicals gained control of Georgia's congressional delegation while the conservatives were left to govern the state without the opposition of the radicals' two most influential leaders.

Soon Georgia became a "state" to be governed. In early March armed conflict broke out, and Governor Wright, along with the last vestiges of royal authority, sailed away. To fill the vacuum, the conservative-dominated provincial congress drew up the "Rules and Regulations of 1776" as a foundation for Georgia's new government. Brief in form, this document did little more than formalize the existing situation, authorizing the provincial congress and the Council of Safety to continue functioning as they had. Thus home rule was established without having to face the partisan question of the exact nature of the government. Yet the "Rules and Regulations" were adopted solely as a temporary measure, and it was only a matter of time before the consensus would be tested again.

With revolution a reality and the rhetoric of revolution the property of all, conservatives rallied in support of the new government. Soon they discovered, if they had not known all along, that the "Rules and Regulations" created a political situation similar to the one they initially sought, and concluded that there was no need to alter it substantially. With power resting in a conservative-controlled legislature, free from executive checks, their goals had been reached. For the conservatives the revolution, in a political sense, was over; for the radicals it was only the beginning.

While conservatives basked in their apparent victory, radicals

VIEW OF SAVANNAH, 1837

In this painting by Joseph Louis Firmin Cerveau, Tondee's Tavern, where independence-minded colonists met to plot their course of action, is indicated by the arrow at upper right. The monument to Revolutionary War hero General Nathanael Greene, the cornerstone of which was laid by General LaFayette on March 20, 1825, is shown in what is now Johnson Square on Bull Street (left center).

continued to curry popular favor, waiting for the opportunity to wield their rapidly growing strength. That moment came in late summer, 1776, when Georgia learned of the Declaration of Independence. Now there was no need to pacify the conservatives lest they desert the movement: For both factions there was no turning back. Aware of this and confident in their role as leaders of the Popular Party, radicals set out to destroy the power of the conservatives.

The opening of the radical attack can be linked directly to the return to Georgia of Button Gwinnett. Fresh from signing the Declaration, he came home prepared to be appointed general of the newly-formed Georgia brigade, but conservative allies in Congress blocked his election. This thwarting of the "popular will" (and of Gwinnett's military ambitions) strengthened the radicals' resolve and set the stage for what was to be the pivotal election of Georgia's revolutionary era.

With independence declared and Congress directing states to put their governments in order, the call went out for an election of a new provincial congress that, among other things, was to serve as a convention for writing a permanent constitution. At that moment all pretense of consensus was abandoned. Conservatives hoped to establish a permanent government similar to the existing one while the radicals planned to frame a constitution that would give more power to an expanded electorate, the Popular Party, and themselves. Neither radical nor conservative saw the need for incorporating the opposition or their ideas into the new government.

The election was one of the most bitterly partisan in Georgia history. Charges and countercharges flew as radicals branded conservatives Tories, conservatives raised spectres of radical anarchy, and in at least one instance violence erupted at the ballot box. But in the end the weight of numbers held sway, and, when the delegates assembled, the Popular Party underscored its newly-won majority by electing Gwinnett as speaker and by placing other radicals in key positions. After months of waiting and maneuvering the struggle seemed nearing its end.

Now it was up to the radicals to formalize their victory. Gwinnett headed the radical-dominated committee charged with drawing up the state's first constitution, and, though most of the records are lost, there is little doubt that the document's final form reflected his views. A directly elected, one-house assembly led the government, with little to check its power except a veto-less executive and his council, both chosen by the legislature. Representatives were to be selected from newly-created counties, under a system which gave Liberty County, dominated by what had been St. John's Parish, a slight numerical advantage over Chatham County, formerly Christ Church.

Along with age and residence requirements, it was stipulated that to vote a man needed only £10 taxable property or to be engaged in a mechanic's trade, requirements liberal enough to open the suffrage to most adult male Georgians. But in holding offices above the county level the radicals were not so confident in the people. One had to own 250 acres of land or £250 of property to stand for election to the assembly — a more open requirement but hardly democratic. Nevertheless, it was a government close to the people, filled with the political ideas and ideals of the Enlightenment, the very existence of which signaled a conservative defeat. The Constitution of 1777 did not end the factional struggle in revolutionary Georgia, but it so redefined the conditions under which it was to be fought that, politically, Georgia would never be the same again. To many it was a symbol of what the revolution was all about — home rule, popular control, and wider political opportunity — but to the radicals it was much more. To them it verified the end of a system that for nearly two decades had held them in a condition of second-class citizenship.

Yet to achieve their victory the radicals had to do more than destroy; they had to create. It was through their creating that the real revolution in Georgia took place. Naturally the expulsion of the British was a revolution as was, for that matter, the overthrow of the conservatives, but the means by which the latter was accomplished — the formation of the Popular Party — gave to Georgia's revolution a deeper significance. Not only did the political system change (though one could argue with some justification that it did not change that much), but, more importantly, the "popular" victory also marked a change in the source from which the government drew its authority to govern.

"The legislature of this state shall be composed of the people," declared the constitution, and with that statement Georgia entered a new political era. By capitalizing on their anti-authoritarian image and by casting their opposition as men bent on thwarting the popular will, radical leaders had been able to draw the "people" to their side. Perhaps, as one historian noted in another context, they never really championed the cause of the people but only invited the people to champion theirs; even if such were the case, though, the "people" refused to be used solely for radical ends. The conservative downfall was as much their victory as a victory for the men of St. John's. Radical overtures raised expectations which had to be fulfilled, and the Constitution of 1777 marks the beginning of that fulfillment.

For better or for worse, popular government was coming to Georgia. A wider political and social stratum was gaining access to the machinery of government; and the attainment of those ideals earlier expounded in the Declaration of Independence — man's "inalienable rights . . . life, liberty, and the pursuit of happiness" — were coming closer to fruition.

This article originally appeared in *The Georgia Historical Quarterly,* Volume LIX (Winter 1975), pp. 388-401, under the title "Consensus and Conflict: Factional Politics in Revolutionary Georgia, 1774-1777." It is used here, with slight modification, by permission of that publication.

Chapter III

LYMAN HALL

James Harvey Young

F ive physicians signed the Declaration of Independence, two from New Hampshire, one from Connecticut, one from Pennsylvania (the notable Benjamin Rush), and one from Georgia, Lyman Hall. Of the long odyssey which took Hall to Pennsylvania's State House in 1776, some parts of his pathway are clearly marked while others are obscure. Fire from torches of British troops, as well as accidental flames, destroyed pertinent records relating to Hall's life. Major documentary searches launched by the National Archives and the Library of Congress during the bicentennial did not discover anything significantly new about Lyman Hall. Nor does an authentic portrait of him exist. His widow and his one child, an unmarried son, did not long survive him. Hall as a person does not emerge with vivid roundness from the accounts of his contemporaries, nor does much information survive about his medical practice. The record amply documents, however, the fervor of Hall's zeal for the political independence of British America.

Historian Ulrich B. Phillips once wrote that "had not a

group of New England families established themselves about the middle of the coast line Georgia might not have joined in the demand for American independence." Lyman Hall was one of these New Englanders. Born of ancient Puritan stock in Wallingford, Connecticut, in 1724, Hall joined a family committed to Congregationalism and to education. His grandfather, a Harvard graduate, and an uncle, a Yale graduate, served as pastors of Wallingford churches. Young Lyman chose to attend Yale, where the president himself tutored Hall in metaphysics and divinity. Studying further with his uncle, Hall himself became a minister at a church riven by doctrinal disputes. Shortly he was charged with immoral conduct, a charge to which he admitted. (The details of Hall's conduct remain unknown because the records, contained within the minister's home, were burned by British troops during the Revolution.) Although dismissed from his pastorate, he was later restored to good standing as a minister. Filling vacant pulpits and also teaching school, though, evidently proved unrewarding to Hall. Therefore, after studying medicine by apprenticeship, he became a physician. By now Hall had married twice (his first wife having died within a year). Soon the new doctor, accompanied by his new wife, departed Connecticut for South Carolina.

The reasons for this relocation are unknown. Perhaps Hall wanted to shake the dust of frustration from his feet. Perhaps he felt his fortunes as a physician might be better served in a less crowded environment. Perhaps a sense of religious mission obsessed him, for, according to tradition, Hall migrated to Dorchester, upriver from Charleston, where for over half a century New England Puritans had maintained a covenanted Congregational society. More likely, Hall settled in Charleston and established a medical practice.

The Halls did not stay in Charleston long. Within several years they joined a new migration by members of the

Dorchester society to Georgia, where restraints upon land ownership had recently been relaxed. The migrants established the Midway settlement, and, in 1760, Hall was granted land for a plantation, "Hall's Knoll," not far from the Midway Meeting House. On his plantation Hall grew rice, and from it he went forth to tend the sick of the community. When his neighbors established the port city of Sunbury on a bluff above the Medway River, Hall built a home there on a lot fronting the bay. He did not stay in Georgia long, however, for by mid-1762 he was back in South Carolina. In the village of Pon Pon, south of Charleston, he advertised himself as a "practitioner of physic and surgery" who also had various medicines, family remedies, perfuming waters, and a "famous cosmetic water." During this period of residence in South Carolina Dr. Hall did not give up "Hall's Knoll" or his Sunbury residence, and by 1774 he was back in Georgia, deeply involved in the politics of revolution.

The year 1774 marked a bitter peak in a decade of increasing tension between mother country and colonies, witnessing the Intolerable Acts and the convening of the First Continental Congress. Alone among the thirteen colonies, Georgia sent no delegates to Philadelphia. Many factors encouraged in Georgians a sense of loyalty to Britain and caution as to words and deeds of protest. Georgia, as the newest colony, had been treated generously by the Parliament with annual grants. British restraints on colonial trade, so disturbing to northern colonies, hardly affected Georgia at all. Indeed, Britain paid high bounties on Georgia's indigo and rice. Hostile Indians, fairly near to every Georgia settlement, remained generally peaceful because of British gifts and troops. Sir James Wright, the royal governor, an able man with colonial interests much at heart, enjoyed wide popularity.

Still, despite such grounds for loyalty, Georgians felt increasing disquiet over developing British policy. In respectful terms the Assembly protested new revenue measures. In 1765, Savannah artisans and small merchants organized the Sons of Liberty and warned of trouble should the Stamp Act be enforced. Through the ensuing years, though, Georgia's responses came more tardily and in a milder form than those from colonies to the north.

When the call for a Continental Congress came in 1774, patriots from every parish assembled at the "liberty pole" in front of Tondee's Tavern and condemned British policy, although majority sentiment opposed sending representatives to the Continental Congress. This do-nothing policy upset patriot leaders from St. John's Parish (Lyman Hall among them), which had sent the largest delegation to the Savannah meeting. Back home in Midway they continued efforts to have Georgia represented in Philadelphia. At local meetings Hall was in fact chosen to go, but he did not do so — probably because he was aware he could not truly represent sentiment in Georgia.

Governor Wright strove busily to stem disloyal sentiment. He spoke of the Sons of Liberty as "Sons of Licentiousness" and condemned the Congregationalists at Midway. This group, the governor wrote, "chiefly descendants of New-England people of the Puritan sect," despite their long residence in the South, retained "a strong tincture of Republican or Oliverian principles" — a reference, of course, to Oliver Cromwell. Wright pointed the finger of blame directly at Lyman Hall.

Already in correspondence with members of the Continental Congress, Hall strove to get Georgia to comply with the Continental Association, by which the Congress sought to curtail trade with Britain. When the first provincial congress in Georgia failed to take this step, the Midway patriots moved to the brink of secession. Interest as well as principle was involved. Adherents to the Continental Association had pledged to cut off trade with those colonies

that did not join, and, in May 1775, the Continental Congress took this step with respect to Georgia. Such a boycott, the planters and merchants of Midway and Sunbury feared, threatened them with economic disaster. They cut off trade with the rest of Georgia and, in a letter signed, and presumably written, by Hall, sought an alliance with the Committee of Correspondence in Charleston that would permit a continuation of trade, even though this might require detaching St. John's Parish from Georgia. But the Charleston patriots would not agree. St. John's remained affixed to Georgia and had to share the consequences of the trade embargo.

St. John's decided to appeal its case to the Continental Congress itself, choosing Lyman Hall to go as spokesman. Hall probably went to Philadelphia by ship, taking with him two hundred barrels of rice collected by the Georgia patriots to give — in Governor Wright's ironic phrase — to "the poor distressed, innocent brethren in Boston," where fighting had begun. On May 13, the Second Continental Congress accorded Hall the status of a delegate, and thus for the next four months the Congress consisted of representatives from twelve colonies and one parish. In September 1775, a second provincial congress, reflecting increasingly radical sentiment in the southern-most colony, elected Hall and two other delegates as Georgia's representatives to the Philadelphia assembly.

While the sole Georgian at the Continental Congress, Hall played a retiring role. He served on a scientific committee, along with John Adams, Benjamin Franklin, and Patrick Henry, to determine the best methods of finding and refining lead and of making salt. The intensifying conflict thus forced upon the Congress an increasing array of practical concerns.

During the early months of 1776, American sentiment accelerated toward the crucial step of revolution. George III spoke of rebellion; British troops bombarded Norfolk; Thomas Paine penned his fiery pamphlet *Common Sense*. Georgia shared in this bold trend. When British men-of-war entered the Savannah River, patriots arrested Governor Wright, paroled him, then saw him flee to the British ships. A brief river battle occurred as the British sought to capture boats loaded with rice. In this atmosphere the new provincial congress elected Hall, Gwinnett, and Walton to go to Philadelphia. Gwinnett had been Hall's neighbor and patient as well as his political ally.

The Georgia delegates came to the Continental Congress with elastic instructions, broad enough to cover concurring in a declaration of independence.

On July 1, John Adams penned a letter to Archibald Bulloch, president of Georgia's provincial congress. "This morning is assigned for the greatest debate of all," Adams wrote. "A declaration, that these colonies are free and independent states, has been reported by a committee appointed some weeks ago for that purpose, and this day or to-morrow is to determine its fate. . . .Your colleagues, Hall and Gwinnett," Adams informed Bulloch, "are here in good health and spirits, and as firm as you yourself could wish them." The Georgia delegation indeed supported the Declaration with firm conviction. They demurred only from that part of Jefferson's draft that condemned King George for continuing the foreign slave trade, a clause the Georgians helped to get deleted.

Through the crucial year 1776, Hall served on a number of committees, some concerned with the health of the Continental Army. He joined a committee to look into the provision of medicines for the troops. As fighting intensified, Congress created special committees aimed at securing drugs, clothing, and other provisions for the wounded and disabled. Hall was appointed to these, sometimes collaborating with Benjamin Rush. Hall also pondered broader matters of policy. He served on a committee that conferred for a week with General Washington and his aides about military plans for the forthcoming campaign. He inquired into the reason for the lack of military success in the Canadian invasion. He wrestled with problems of finding ways to get more money into the treasury.

Lyman Hall, although steadily re-elected from Georgia to the Continental Congress through 1780, made his last appearance there in February 1777. His absence did not indicate lack of interest. Instead, it meant that the state scene took precedence for him over Confederation business. "I frequently Wish to be with you," he wrote a Connecticut delegate, "but Alas! this state is in so much Danger Externally & Internally that it seems Necessary that I should Throw my Small Might for its preservation." Georgia adopted a state constitution of which Hall was inordinately proud.

Hall was present in Savannah when the first Assembly met to elect a governor. The rivalry was intense, for Georgia patriots had split into two bitter factions, one rural, liberal, and wary of military dominance over civil affairs, the other urban, conservative, and respectful of the military. Hall favored Gwinnett's candidacy, but Gwinnett lost. Hall was present in the chamber, but he was not close enough to hear the scurrilous remark by General Lachlan McIntosh that led to the famous duel between the two. At Gwinnett's death, Hall wrote a member of the Continental Congress: "O Liberty! Why do you suffer so many faithful sons; your warmest Votaries, to fall at your Shrine! Alas! my Friend, my Friend!"

Late in 1778, the British began to apply the strategy of trying to win the war by first conquering the South. They recaptured Savannah in December and soon regained control of the rest of Georgia except for some frontier areas. Governor Wright returned to govern, staying until the British evacuated Savannah in June 1782. St. John's Parish, made the nucleus of Liberty County under the first state organization, bore the brunt of British revenge, because here revolutionary fervor had burned the brightest. As British regulars and American Tories ravaged the coastal region, the plantation house at "Hall's Knoll" and Dr. Hall's home in Sunbury went up in flames. Named in a British act of attainder, Hall stood accused of high treason, his property confiscated. Anticipating such disasters, he moved his family, first to the vicinity of Charleston, then probably to shelter with relatives in Connecticut.

The Halls returned to Georgia when the British had gone. After establishing a medical practice in Savannah, Dr. Hall

LYMAN HALL

set about recovering his land in Liberty County. From that constituency he was chosen to the House of Assembly of the state. The legislature met in January 1783 and as its first act called Hall away from medicine once more to political service by electing him governor. In notifying him of this honor, the speaker praised him for the "Early and decided Part" he had taken "in the cause of america" and for "exertions in the Course of the Arduous and important Struggle Which Preceeded the Auspicious dawn of Independence."

The state of Georgia faced massive problems, and as a "reconstruction" governor Hall wrestled with them manfully. Although peace negotiations were under way, the war had not ended. The coast lay vulnerable to renewed attack. Tories made forays from across the Florida border. Within Georgia bandits preyed upon honest citizens. The Creeks and the Cherokee, spurred on by the British and Spanish and angered by the intrusions of land-hungry frontiersmen, posed trouble. Amidst the war's devastation, crops had been neglected, and starvation threatened. Often during Hall's year as governor the state treasury stood, as the Executive Council once described it, "at present altogether empty."

Faced with such massive problems, Governor Hall sought actively to take what steps his weak executive authority permitted. He tried to maintain adequate defense and provision the troops. He pushed rigorously a policy of exiling troublesome Tories and confiscating their estates. New land cessions from the Indians were sought to reward soldiers and lure more settlers to the state. He led parlays for this purpose with both the Cherokee and the Creeks. He tried, largely in vain, to reorder the state's shakey finances. One of his final gubernatorial acts was to inform Georgians of the treaty signed in Paris officially ending the war.

Governor Hall thought also in terms of mental and spiritual reconstruction. He urged the Assembly to consider a broad and perceptive list of policies. "Blessings [such as peace], unless improved," he asserted, "change their nature; and neglected, will involve us in the severest calamities." He suggested laws restraining vice, encouraging religion, and supporting education. The legislature heeded Hall's words and set aside land to subsidize academies in three of the state's towns. Moreover, the governor's suggestion, boldly built upon by another Yale graduate, Hall's friend Abraham Baldwin, led to the chartering of Franklin College (University of Georgia).

In time Hall sold "Hall's Knoll", but he retained an interest in plantation economy. In 1789, he joined with like-minded men in forming a society for the promotion of agriculture. The next year he retired from his medical practice in Savannah to another plantation he bought in Burke County on a bluff overlooking the Savannah River. He lived there only a few months, dying in 1790 at the age of sixty-six.

Lyman Hall was a tall man for his time, six feet one inch; he was courteous and dignified, mild and generally calm of temper. When the times required, though, he became a fearless champion of independence, singled out invidiously by the king's governor. As events pushed him into greater prominence, he acquired a modicum of political ambition, a taste for office. He willingly represented his parish, then all of Georgia, in the Continental Congress and later accepted the governorship with alacrity. Powerful ambition, however, does not seem to have been part of his makeup. In the Congress he performed as a steady committeeman, not a major leader, seldom participating in debate. As governor he tended diligently to business and possessed a broad grasp of Georgia's problems as a newly-independent state. His New England heritage helped turn colonial Georgia toward independence and helped turn the new state of Georgia towards matters of the mind and spirit.

A Note on Sources

Primary sources for the most prominent events in which Lyman Hall played a part have been assembled in such useful collections as Worthington C. Ford, ed., *Journals of the Continental Congress* (Washington, 1904-1937); Edmund C. Burnett, ed., *Letters of Members of the Continental Congress* (Washington, 1921-1936); Allen D. Candler, compiler, *The Revolutionary Records of the State of Georgia* (Atlanta, 1908); and George White, ed., *Historical Collections of Georgia* (New York, 1854). The *Gazettes* of Savannah and Charleston added a few items of interest to the record.

The best biographical sketch of Hall appears in Charles C. Jones, Jr., *Biographical Sketches of the Delegates from Georgia to the Continental Congress* (Boston, 1891), although the chronology of his life in South Carolina and Georgia required revision. James W. Hall, *Lyman Hall, Georgia Patriot* (Savannah, 1959), a labor of love, although not by a relative, contains some new material. Shorter summaries include Franklin B. Dexter, *Biographical Sketches of the Graduates of Yale College* (New York, 1896), II, 116-19; Herbert Thoms, "Lyman Hall, Physician, Patriot, 'Signer'," *Medical Journal and Record* (1927); and Joseph Krafka, Jr., "Lyman Hall — Yale 1747," *Yale Journal of Biology and Medicine* (1938). Useful background studies are Jack C. Crandall, "Georgia and the Continental Congress" (unpublished master's thesis, Emory University, 1949), and Kenneth Coleman, *The American Revolution in Georgia, 1763-1789* (Athens, 1958).

Aid was generously given by Rick Beard, then of the National Portrait Gallery, David R. Chesnutt and George C. Rogers, Jr., of the University of South Carolina, Kenneth Coleman of the University of Georgia, Sandra B. Groover of the Georgia Department of Archives and History, Howard R. Lamar of Yale University, and James Z. Rabun of Emory University.

This sketch of the life of Lyman Hall is an abbreviated version of a longer essay entitled "Lyman Hall, A Connecticut Yankee in Georgia," which appeared in the March April 1976 issue of the *Harvard Medical Alumni Bulletin* and in *Physician Signers of the Declaration of Independence*, published in 1976 by Science History Publications, New York. The special issue of the *Bulletin* and the book were both edited by the late George E. Gifford, Jr. Permission was granted for republication in this form by Dr. Gifford and has been granted also by the editors of the *Harvard Medical Alumni Bulletin* and of Science History Publications.

Chapter IV

BUTTON GWINNETT

Harvey H. Jackson

Although he was one of Georgia's revolutionary leaders, a member of the Continental Congress, chief executive of the state, and a signer of the Declaration of Independence, most people today know little about Button Gwinnett. Ironically, his main claim to fame is largely responsible for that situation: His signature is the rarest of the Declaration's signers.

We know so little of him because he left little behind to tell the tale. To make matters worse, the few surviving records that might shed some light on the man and his work were produced by either enthusiastic supporters or bitter enemies, and are therefore filled with contradictions. Was Gwinnett, as family and friends insisted, a man "so attatched to the Liberty of [his] State & Continent, that his whole Attention[,] Influence[,] & Interest, centered in it"? Or was he the "dictator" fellow signer George Walton attacked as a "rotten hearted[,] designing enemy," whose "trumped up" accusations "no gentleman could have suffered long"? With such conflicting sources it is no wonder that most studies of his life have been fragmented and often biased.

There was, however, one point on which his contemporaries — friend and foe — clearly agreed, and that point will be the focus of this essay. For better or for worse, Button Gwinnett was, as his close friend (and another Georgia signer) Lyman Hall assessed him, "if possible a Whig to Excess."

Born in England in 1735, the second son of a Gloucestershire vicar, Button Gwinnett grew up in a household that served the local gentry but was only an incidental part of it. He benefited from a better-than-average education and from family connections that gave him the opportunity to pursue a mercantile career. As a young man he was involved in a variety of business ventures in and around Bristol; but he found prospects so unpromising that, in the early 1760s, he left his native land (and his creditors) and set sail for America. During the next few years commercial activities carried him as far south as Jamaica and as far north as Newfoundland, but still success eluded him. This period, like so much of his life, is shrouded in mystery. All that remains is a rather unsavory account of his relations with a Philadelphia merchant, which leaves the distinct impression that Button Gwinnett was an opportunist interested only in Button Gwinnett. It was not the last time such a charge was raised.

These wanderings ended in 1765, when the future signer appeared in Savannah, rented a store, and announced the arrival of Button Gwinnett, *Merchant.* His timing could not have been worse. With the colony's economy near chaos over the Stamp Act, and the local commercial community anything but receptive to new competition, his venture failed. But Button Gwinnett was adaptable — let that be his character note. Turning his back on Savannah, he borrowed the money to buy St. Catherines Island in St. John's Parish. Undaunted by his lack of experience, Button Gwinnett,

Merchant, resolved to become Button Gwinnett, *Planter.*

Soon after arriving, his interests turned from planting to politics — a calling for which he proved far better prepared. In fact, the one description of him that could have come from an eyewitness, set down by the early Georgia historian Hugh McCall, pictures a man well suited for the public arena.

> He was about six feet in height, and his person was properly proportioned, lofty and commanding. Without possessing remarkable eloquence his language was mild and persuasive. His manners were polite and his deportment graceful.

In Gwinnett the citizens of St. John's Parish discovered a new leader, and soon local offices, such as Justice of the Peace, came his way. This recognition culminated in 1769 in his being chosen to serve in the Commons House of Assembly, the legislative body in which sat Georgia's rising colonial elite.

Prior to Gwinnett's election the Commons had been attempting to expand its power at the expense of the royal governor, James Wright, with little success. That struggle was moving into another phase when the new legislator arrived to take his seat. Quickly assessing the situation, Gwinnett sided with the governor's opponents and, despite his "freshman" status, emerged as a spokesman for the Commons' position opposing taxing parishes not represented in the Assembly. His appointment to the committee charged with drafting and presenting a "Humble Address" to the governor on the matter made it obvious that his colleagues saw him as anything but a political novice. Button Gwinnett seemed on the brink of a long and illustrious legislative career.

Then, as rapidly as he rose, he fell. Proving even less adept at planting than business, Gwinnett watched his debts grow and his resources shrink. Hounded by creditors, he abandoned the Assembly after one session, never to return. From that point his efforts reveal a desperate man, struggling to stave off bankruptcy and, at times, stretching legality to its limit. Nothing worked. Finally, in 1773, his personal property was attached and sold, and soon St. Catherines went on the block. By the eve of the revolution Button Gwinnett seemed just another of the many who sought their fortune in Georgia and failed.

Revolutionaries seldom rise from the ranks of the contented, though, and the most volatile are the ambitious whose ambitions are thwarted. Gwinnett came to America seeking what England denied him — prosperity and status. When Savannah, and circumstances, frustrated his initial efforts, he turned to St. John's Parish, which welcomed him with open arms. There, politically at least, he found success and briefly enjoyed the standing he sought. Then he lost it, not because he was a poor politician, but because he was a poor businessman. In Georgia, as in most colonies, few who failed at business could hope to succeed at politics.

Despite his problems Button Gwinnett refused to give up. Instead, he lay part of (if not all) the blame for what had befallen him on those lawyers, merchants, and planters with whom he dealt and on the system that enabled them to control his life. This inclination and the methods later used to redress these real and imagined grievances were to make him one of Georgia's most controversial revolutionary leaders. During this time he held to what he could, maintained his political connections, and waited for his chance. When it came, he was ready.

The events that led to Gwinnett's political resurrection were set in motion during the summer of 1774, when Georgia Whigs (as supporters of American rights were called) met to protest Britain closing the port of Boston in retaliation for the "tea party." At these gatherings divisions appeared that threatened to destroy this movement almost before it began.

On one side was a coalition representing areas from which the colony's traditional leadership had come — Savannah, surrounding Christ Church Parish, and some of the older regions of the province. Having failed in earlier attempts to expand their power by expanding that of the Commons (which they controlled), this group hoped to use reaction to the new British outrages to discredit Governor Wright and bring him to their terms. To them, the political system that could best protect Georgians' liberties was one in which the legislature was supreme, for they were supreme in the legislature.

Opposing the Christ Church coalition were Whigs from St. John's Parish. Settled largely by Puritans whose search for a new Zion carried them from Massachusetts to South Carolina in the 1690s, and finally to Georgia in the 1750s, St. John's boasted a plantation system to rival older areas and the town of Sunbury, Georgia's second port of entry. But the parish was not able to translate economic accomplishments into political power, for in colonial Georgia the Christ Church coalition led and the rest followed. Exactly why these Puritans found this arrangement so burdensome, even threatening, is a question for which there is no simple answer; but it is sufficient to say that Whigs from St. John's saw little future for themselves in a movement dominated by the Christ Church coalition. Therefore, the men from St. John's concluded that their liberties could not be defended simply by reducing the power of the royal governor. To be truly free, they would have to reduce the power of the Christ Church coalition as well.

Although no Puritan, the bankrupt Button Gwinnett was in sympathy with his parish's position and shared its ultimate objectives. Finding himself at the mercy of the men who directed the colony's economy (who were also the men who led the Christ Church coalition), it was simple to lay the blame for his condition at their feet. It then followed that if the Christ Church coalition was the source of his problem, to reduce its power would benefit not only the colony but Button Gwinnett as well. He and his friends from St. John's may have traveled different routes, but they arrived at the same place, at the same time.

There is no record that Gwinnett attended the meetings in Savannah in the summer of 1774 or the local gatherings held after the Whigs split over sending delegates to the Continental Congress. Understandably, he was not at the first provincial congress, called by Christ Church, for it was boycotted by St. John's. Surprisingly, Gwinnett was also absent when the two factions, having discovered they could not succeed unless they cooperated, united in a second provincial congress in July 1775. Yet the future signer was not idle. He was hard at work for the Whig cause, for St. John's, and for Button Gwinnett. Instead of operating within the newly-formed united front, he set out to create a St. John's-led coalition that would break the power of Christ Church and its allies once and for all. What he accomplished changed the course of the American Revolution in Georgia.

While the second provincial congress was meeting, Gwinnett was at work in the back country, where he organized a "nocturnal Cabal" . . . and by his address and management persuaded many of the members, both to the southward and to the westward . . . that the views and interests of [Christ Church Parish and] the town of Savannah were different from those of the State." That he did this (as detractors later claimed) "with a manifest intention to set one part of the province at variance and enmity with the other" is debatable, but the fact that such was the result is not.

Appealing to east-west and city-rural tensions that had existed for most of the colonial period, Button Gwinnett was able to fashion a political alliance between Whigs from St. John's and a collection of rural individuals and interests

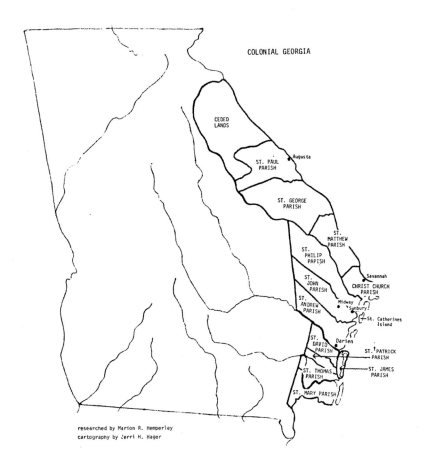

COLONIAL GEORGIA

CEDED
LANDS

ST. PAUL
PARISH

● Augusta

ST. GEORGE
PARISH

ST.
MATTHEW
PARISH

ST.
PHILIP
PAPISH

ST.
JOHN
PARISH

ST.
ANDREW
PARISH

● Savannah

CHRIST CHURCH
PARISH

Midway ●
Sunbury!

St. Catherines
Island

ST.
DAVID
PARISH

Darien

ST. PATRICK
PARISH

ST. THOMAS
PARISH

ST. JAMES
PARISH

ST. MARY PARISH

researched by Marion R. Hemperley
cartography by Jerri H. Hager

MAP OF COLONIAL GEORGIA

generally dubbed the "western members." Promising, among other things, a political system more open to participation by the average Georgian and more responsive to his needs, Gwinnett proposed, in effect, to replace the Christ Chruch elite, which dominated the government, with men who represented the majority of the people. Whether he actually advocated "democracy" is debatable; but what his followers (and his enemies) believed the outcome would be was expressed in the name the movement came to be called — the Popular Party.

In January 1776, the Popular Party got its first test. The Continental Congress had authorized a continental battalion raised in Georgia, with its commander selected by the legislature. Realizing the power and prestige accompanying the position, the Christ Church coalition nominated one of their own, Samuel Elbert: Equally aware of the significance of the post, St. John's countered by nominating Button Gwinnett. In the past Elbert's election would have been little more than a formality, but things had changed. The "western members" rose to the occasion, refused to accept Savannah's choice, and rallied around their new hero. When the votes were counted, Button Gwinnett, "without any one military qualification," was declared elected.

This show of strength, though impressive, was premature. With Governor Wright still in the colony, and many of the more conservative Whigs fearing matters were getting out of hand, it was not the time to risk a defection. A compromise was struck. Gwinnett withdrew to join his friend Lyman Hall in the Continental Congress; Elbert was appointed lieutenant colonel of the battalion; and command went to Lachlan McIntosh of Darien. Leader of a prominent south Georgia family, a planter and local politician with ties to Savannah, St. John's, and the southern parishes, McIntosh was as close to a neutral as might be found in the faction-beset colony. He was acceptable to most and objectionable to none — at least not yet.

On May 20, 1776, Button Gwinnett presented his credentials to the Continental Congress. In the time between his election and his arrival in Philadelphia, fighting had broken out in Georgia, Governor Wright had fled, and the state was being governed by the provincial congress under an admittedly temporary constitution called the "Rules and Regulations of 1776." Equally important, by the time Gwinnett took his seat, the provincial congress was once again under the control of the Christ Church coalition. Fear of an invasion by Loyalists based in Florida, and by Loyalist-led Indians, brought many frontier Whigs back to their traditional leaders. This allegiance was conditioned on the coalition's ability to defend Georgia, and at that they had little success. Unable to supply McIntosh the men and supplies needed or to co-ordinate civil and military operations, the Christ Church-led government hindered the war effort as much as it helped. Reports of this reached Philadelphia, colored no doubt by partisan embellishments, and convinced Gwinnett that changes had to be made — and that he was the one to make them.

For the moment, though, Gwinnett had other concerns. His credentials accepted, he was appointed to serve on a number of committees, including one charged with studying plans for a confederation of the states. He was also instrumental in securing a $60,000 appropriation for the defense of Georgia, and he favored granting the Continental Congress power to regulate Indian affairs and trade — a stand which probably reflected his concern for Georgia's frontier defenses, rather than his support for a strong national government. No record remains to reveal that he took part in the debates over independence, but, on July 2, he voted to accept the resolution calling for separation. On July 4, he signed a draft of the Declaration, and, on August 2, 1776, he added his name to the final copy. With that his work in Philadelphia was done, and he began the long journey back to Georgia.

It has been generally assumed Gwinnett expected the Continental Congress to select him to lead the newly-created Georgia brigade, so he returned home to be ready to take command when the news reached him. But if the brigade was his major concern, why did he leave Philadelphia a month before the commander was chosen? As there was little he could do militarily until the commission arrived, why did he not remain at the Congress, use his influence to assure his selection, and then return as General Gwinnett? By failing to do so he allowed his enemies in Philadelphia to block his appointment and put Lachlan McIntosh in his place. For the second time McIntosh had come between Gwinnett and the power and prestige of a military command, an occurrence the signer could not be expected to overlook.

Button Gwinnett had a very good reason for returning when he did — a reason that, on balance, far outweighed his military ambition. About the time Gwinnett left Congress, Archibald Bulloch, president of Georgia's Council of Safety, called for the election of a "Convention" that, his proclamation strongly implied, would act on an earlier congressional resolution and write a permanent constitution for the state. Gwinnett and other state leaders surely anticipated this announcement, and his decision to return when he did seems hardly accidental. Other states were answering Congress' call; and other signers, including Thomas Jefferson, were leaving Philadelphia, convinced that within the framing of these new governments revolutionary ideology would become reality. Though self-interest cannot be divorced from his motives, Button Gwinnett had a vision of a new Georgia, one in which the people had a greater voice in decisions affecting their lives, liberty, and property. He returned to make that dream reality.

Using the Christ Church coalition's inability to defend the

frontiers as a whipping boy, Gwinnett and his corps of
dedicated followers raised issues — equal representation and
popular participation — that were critical concerns. From the
beginning the Popular Party enjoyed a significant advantage
and, guided by Button Gwinnett, exploited it to the fullest.
The Christ Church coalition had little with which to counter.
Their military record was indeed poor (though this was not
entirely their fault), and, despite a willingness to re-apportion
the provincial congress to some extent, they were hardly
willing to go as far as the Popular Party wanted. With little to
offer as an alternative, the coalition could only belittle the
notion of popular govenment, which insulted the very people
whose support they needed. Increasingly suspicious of this
new political force, fearful of its motives, and less than willing
to cooperate with its leaders or acknowledge the legitimacy
of its goals, the coalition found themselves supporting the old
order just as the new was emerging. They were beaten
before the ballots were counted.

Despite the near certainty of the outcome, the election was still
one of the most bitterly contested in Georgia's history. More
than a mandate for or against a military policy (although popular
perception of who could best defend the state was crucial to the
outcome), the results determined who would write the rules
under which future governments would govern — rules that
could also determine who would govern as well. Thus, when the
Popular Party carried the day, the man selected speaker of the
convention, and charged with translating rhetoric into reality,
was Button Gwinnett. At least some of the disappointment he
felt at losing the brigade to McIntosh was surely salved.

Because only a small part of the convention's journal has
survived, it is impossible to say exactly when work on the
constitution began; but by December the writing seems to have
been underway. Not surprisingly, Speaker Gwinnett headed the
committee selected to draft the document, and the other
members (none identifiable as from Christ Church) were surely

his choices. On January 29, 1777, the constitution was debated in its final form, and on February 5, it was passed without a dissenting vote. What remained of the Christ Church coalition either bowed to the inevitable or abstained.

The resulting document was nothing short of revolutionary. In addition to generally lowering voter qualifications and creating a single-house legislature, along with a weak executive, the new constitution replaced the parish system that allowed Christ Church to dominate the government with counties, drawn so as to more nearly reflect population distribution in the state and give the advantage to the Popular Party. It was hardly the "stark naked democracy" feared by the Christ Church coalition, but it was a significant step in that direction.

Gwinnett's concerns were not limited to Georgia's political situation. Even before work on the constitution began, he and the Popular Party set about to improve the deteriorating military situation. Convinced the state's defense problems stemmed from a lack of resolve on the part of the state's defenders, he and his followers set out to remove those officers whose support for the cause was considered less than vigorous — officers associated with the Christ Church coalition. The purge that followed factionalized what remained of the army's neutrality and in the process put Button Gwinnett on a collision course with General Lachlan McIntosh.

In many ways Lachlan McIntosh was everything Button Gwinnett had wanted to be. Tall, athletic, once described by a friend as the "handsomest man he had ever seen," McIntosh had long enjoyed the economic success, social status, and political prestige that earlier eluded Gwinnett. Furthermore, the general led a family whose influence permeated the Whig movement. His position, combined with that of his older brother, William, a colonel in the horse militia, and his younger brother, George, who served in the provincial congress and on the Council of Safety, made it all but impossible for any matter of substance to escape the notice of the McIntoshes. It also made it difficult for anyone to criticize the government or the army without criticizing the family. Thus, as the Popular Party's attack on the Christ Church coalition grew more intense, accusations spilled over onto the McIntoshes, who responded by denouncing Gwinnett and his friends and joining his enemies.

The first direct confrontation between these new adversaries came in December 1776, when the Popular Party charged that cavalry led by Colonel William McIntosh had deserted the area south of the Altamaha. Because the party now controlled the legislature, and the militia was subject to state authority, Colonel McIntosh had to answer to it for his actions. Although he was ultimately acquitted, the strain of the controversy damaged his health and he resigned, which was probably the purpose of the charges at the outset. Gwinnett's role in all this is obscure, for he was devoting most of his time to the new constitution and apparently left military matters to others. Lachlan McIntosh, however, had no doubts as to who was responsible. The source of his brother's trouble was the Popular Party, and its leader was Button Gwinnett.

Meanwhile, Georgia's military situation seemed to go from bad to worse. As it did, the Christ Church coalition laid the blame at the feet of the now-dominant Popular Party. The new government responded that the fault was not with it, but rather with Loyalists posing as Whigs, who undermined their efforts, and also with the commander of the continental forces, General Lachlan McIntosh, who refused to accept civilian control over the military. Actually, there was more than enough responsibility to go around. McIntosh was reluctant to follow orders from state leaders, not because they were civilian, but because they were members of the Popular Party. On the other hand, the militia was so disrupted by the Popular Party's "purges" that it was hardly an effective force. As for the charge of Tory infiltration, Georgia was indeed noted for divided families and divided loyalties, but it is difficult to say exactly how important that factor actually was. Nevertheless, it was a recurring revolutionary concern, and one

BUTTON GWINNETT

that was about to become more of an issue than ever before.

After the provincial congress adjourned in mid-February, the government was left in the hands of the Council of Safety and its president, Archibald Bulloch. Gwinnett sat on the Council, as did George McIntosh; for the moment an uneasy peace seemed to exist between the factions. Suddenly, late in the month, President Bulloch died. Rumors of poisoning were never proven; and, when the Council met to select a new president, Button Gwinnett was chosen. There was only one vote cast against him — that of George McIntosh. The truce, if indeed there was one, had ended.

On the day of his election, President Gwinnett, whose office also included the responsibilities of commander-in-chief of the militia, was authorized by the Council to lead an expedition against St. Augustine. Headquarters of the Loyalist raiders who plagued the frontier, the Florida capital was in the opinion of many Georgians (especially those outside the Savannah area) the source of all their troubles.

Exactly who suggested the expedition is unclear; but, as Gwinnett emerged as the plan's strongest supporter, there is every reason to believe that the newly-elected chief executive had proposed it to the Council. He certainly had no reason to oppose it. As the expedition's leader he would finally have the military command he had twice been denied, and he would also have the opportunity to rid the state of the most obvious threat to its security; but there was a problem. The militia was not strong enough to carry the burden alone, which meant Gwinnett would need help from the Georgia continental troops. The president's relations with General McIntosh, however, promised little cooperation in that quarter. If continental soldiers were to be part of the expedition, they would have to be found elsewhere.

President Gwinnett put his hopes for additional support on General Robert Howe, commander of the Southern Department, who arrived in Savannah in early March. If Howe would provide the troops, the expedition had some hope of success; and cooperation with McIntosh would be unnecessary. Howe, however, pointedly told Gwinnett that the expedition could not succeed and refused to grant any aid. The president persisted, and Howe finally took to avoiding him entirely, which convinced Gwinnett that the commander was in league with McIntosh and the Christ Church coalition. Simply put, what President Gwinnett wanted was support from the continental troops without having to deal with General McIntosh. In part this position resulted from the growing personal animosity between the two men, but there was also another reason. Button Gwinnett had become convinced that the McIntoshes were more than members of his political opposition; they were traitors to the cause as well.

This opinion was formed on, or soon after, March 14, 1777. On that day President Gwinnett received a packet of documents from John Hancock, president of the Continental Congress. Included in it was a letter from East Florida Royal Governor Patrick Tonyn to Lord George Germain, which had been intercepted by the Americans. The letter was nothing short of a revelation. In it the royal governor described how a Loyalist named William Panton shipped a load of rice from Georgia with the help of "Mr. George McIntosh." George McIntosh was, according to the governor, a man whose "principles [were] a loyal attachment to the King and Constitution," but who was "compelled to a tacit acquiescence with the distemper of the times." Nevertheless, the governor continued, George McIntosh was willing to "be of all the service in his power." Based on such information, the congressional recommendation was no surprise: George McIntosh was to be arrested. Considering his own opinion of the man, Gwinnett's response was hardly surprising either: The recommendation was quickly carried out.

The incident to which Tonyn referred had taken place some ten months earlier. In May 1776, George McIntosh had formed a partnership with his brothers-in-law, Robert Baillie and

Sir Patrick Houstoun, to ship a load of rice to Dutch Guiana. Even this early in the struggle Baillie and Houstoun were suspected of being less than committed to the cause, but because they were "family", McIntosh's association with them in what appeared a legitimate trading venture posed no immediate problem. Before the vessel sailed, the three were joined by Panton, a known Loyalist, who was put in charge of the cargo. He sent the ship to St. Augustine and from there to the British West Indies, a clear violation of the Continental Association. This was a serious matter. For George McIntosh — a prominent member of the government — to engage in trade with a known British supporter like Panton could not be excused simply with the claim that he did not know the rice would be shipped to a British port. This action, plus Tonyn's letter, made it clear to Gwinnett and the Popular Party that George McIntosh was indeed a traitor. They also concluded, although the evidence in this case was hardly so clear, that the other McIntoshes and their relations were "Tories by Consanguinity."

George McIntosh was put in irons and taken to the common jail, an action that was not without precedent, but one that nevertheless outraged his family. Rushing to his brother's aid, General Lachlan McIntosh brushed aside the damaging evidence and instead denounced the president as a man seeking personal and political revenge. Despite the vigor of these charges, there is no evidence that Gwinnett exceeded his authority in the arrest, although it must not have been an unpleasant task to perform. Actually the McIntosh attacks proved counterproductive for they only reinforced the belief, deeply held by members of the Popular Party, that there were many traitors within the Whig ranks. What more proof could one want? Here was a member of the Council who had been condemned by Florida's royal governor, and still his brother, who commanded the continental troops in Georgia, and his friends, many of whom served or had served in the government, rallied to the traitor's defense. What more proof, indeed?

This turn of events finally moved General Howe to meet once again with President Gwinnett; however, the president's suggestion that General McIntosh be transferred because his presence caused Georgians to doubt the loyalty of their army was politely received and ignored. Because there were no charges against the Georgia general, Howe seemed to feel, as did the McIntoshes, that Gwinnett was using the incident as an excuse to rid himself of a powerful opponent. The final blow to Gwinnett's hopes came a few days later when he presented his final plan for the St. Augustine expedition to a still less than receptive General Howe. Once again the proposal was rejected as unnecessary and unworkable. A few days later the commander of the Southern Department announced he was returning to Charleston. "He came," Gwinnett lamented to John Hancock, "he saw, and left us in our low Estate."

About the time Howe left, George McIntosh was released on bail, with four members of the Council of Safety among those who signed his bond. Faced with such divisions in the Whig ranks, and with the rising fear among many that "Toryism" was about to destroy all they had fought for, President Gwinnett decided to proceed with his plan. He was, however, faced with a dilemma. Clearly he needed help from the Georgia continentals, but he did not trust the man who commanded them. Now, with no aid from Howe forthcoming, he would have to go it alone or not go at all. He decided to go it alone.

It was a decision that filled McIntosh with fear. Convinced that Gwinnett would fail, the general concluded that the president planned to blame the failure, when it occurred, on him. However, if the expedition did succeed, McIntosh believed Gwinnett would argue that it proved continental troops were not needed in Georgia, and thus have him removed. Believing this, McIntosh felt he had no choice: He announced that his men would help if asked. Now the long process of watching and waiting began.

Amid all this political intrigue the expedition finally got started, and quickly stopped. Lacking every conceivable military necessity, the militia, most of which came from St. John's Parish, got no farther than Sunbury. Realizing his predicament, the president did the only thing he could: He called on McIntosh. The response, which was anything but enthusiastic, was matched by the welcome the general received when he arrived in Gwinnett's camp. From the start they refused to cooperate, even on the most basic matters; and that situation continued until the Council of Safety, seeing nothing was going to be accomplished, ordered them back to Savannah. The expedition was put under Colonel Samuel Elbert, who made a noble effort to carry it through, but it was hopeless. By mid-June, Georgia's "army" was making its way back to Savannah.

Meanwhile, in the capital, sides were being drawn as differences in politics and philosophy gave way to personal attacks and character assassinations. Lyman Hall had recently returned to the state and was rallying the Popular Party to Gwinnett's defense. At about the same time George Walton, still in Philadelphia, was writing General McIntosh to warn that the president was set on a course to ruin him. To Walton, his fellow signer was a man who made "virtue subservient to his vices [and] to cover the multitude of the latter he affect[ed] to be possessed of the former." In short, Walton observed, Gwinnett would switch factions to suit his aims, was loyal to no one but Lyman Hall, and therefore should be watched with care. It was a warning McIntosh appreciated but really did not need. Already he believed that every word Walton said was true. In Georgia, reason had flown, and neither faction was able to credit the other with motives other than the most base and mean. Expecting the worst from their opponents, both sides were able to find it; and in the end all were guilty.

Matters came to a head in early May, when the first Assembly under the new constitution met to organize the government. One of the first items on the agenda was the election of a governor, which the Assembly was empowered to do. Gwinnett wanted, and indeed expected, the position; but recent charges and counter-charges had identified him with issues and actions too extreme for most Georgians. Apparently hoping to turn the state from the bitter partisanship that had engulfed it, a coalition of moderates from both factions united to elect John Adam Treutlen, a member of the Popular Party who was not closely identified with either Gwinnett or the "western members." Although he was surely disappointed at the turn of events, the former president's wounded pride was salved somewhat when the Assembly investigated the St. Augustine debacle and found that his conduct in the affair had been legal and correct — which, by implication, meant McIntosh's was not. The general was outraged. There, on the floor of the Assembly, with the leaders of Georgia as witnesses, he denounced Button Gwinnett as *"a Scoundrell & Lying Rascal."*

What followed was hardly unexpected. Gwinnett, his political career in limbo, could not accept a public insult to his honor. That same evening, May 15, his written challenge was delivered. In it he asked the general to "give him satisfaction . . . as a gentleman, before sunrise next morning, in Sir James Wright's pasture," which was located just off the Thunderbolt road, about a mile from the center of Savannah. McIntosh, as sensitive of his honor as Gwinnett, "humorously" replied "that the hour was rather earlier than his usual," but he would be at the appointed place, at the appointed time, "with a pair of pistols only." All that remained was to wait out the night.

General McIntosh and his second, Colonel Joseph Habersham, were the first to arrive the next morning. Gwinnett and his second, George Wells, soon joined them. Together the four seemed to personify the whole factional struggle that had brought them to that place. On one side were McIntosh and Habersham — continental officers from old, wealthy, socially prominent, politically powerful families. One could hardly hope to find better representatives of the people who dominated Georgia, the colony, and hoped to dominate Georgia, the state. Standing opposite them, physically and politically, were

Gwinnett and Wells — the former from St. John's, the latter from Augusta. They were the alliance between coastal dissidents and "western members" reduced to its smallest components. It was as if all the social, economic, political, and sectional divisions that marked (and marred) the Whig movement were there in Wright's pasture at dawn on Friday, the 16th of May 1777.

Formal greetings were exchanged and the pistols were loaded, each with a single ball. The principals and their seconds then moved down the hill, out of sight of a group of spectators who had gathered, and the seconds asked what distance should be set. Gwinnett deferred to the general, who coldly suggested that "eight or ten feet should be sufficient." Habersham, feeling that was too close, asked that another step be added. It was, but it made little real difference. Any doubts as to the intent of the parties, especially McIntosh, were dispelled once and for all, when it was proposed that they begin back to back. "By no means," the general responded, "let us see what we are about." This was a blood feud.

The two men took their places, "agreed to fire as they could," and suddenly it was over. Gwinnett fell, his leg broken just above the knee. McIntosh still stood, though his adversary's ball had pierced "the thick of his thigh." Thinking Gwinnett's wound was no worse than his own, the general asked if he would like to exchange another shot. Gwinnett replied that he was willing if the seconds would help him stand. The seconds would not. Declaring that both combatants had "behaved like gentlemen and men of honor," Habersham and Wells refused to allow the duel to continue. Instead, they brought the adversaries together for the ceremonial handshake, then took their wounded charges home.

It was hot that May in 1777, and Gwinnett's condition was aggravated by the sticky, clinging heat that engulfs Savannah in the summer. Over the weekend "a Mortification came on." On Monday morning, May 19, death claimed Button Gwinnett, past president of Georgia, delegate to the Continental Congress, and signer of the Declaration of Independence.

But the movement he helped create, and so ably led, did not die with him. The basic principle upon which his Popular Party was founded — the principle that common people had a right to be more than followers — had become, and would remain, a guiding principle in Georgia politics. Establishing that ideal was no easy task, and the process by which it was accomplished was bitter and divisive.

Button Gwinnett did not create the divisions that existed in colonial and revolutionary Georgia. He recognized them, and he exploited them; but they were already there. More importantly, he turned those divisions into a creative force. The Popular Party, for all its ills and excesses, was Georgia's first truly, and unashamedly, "democratic" movement of any consequence. The Constitution of 1777, which codified the aims and ambitions of that movement, continued to stand, even though its author had fallen.

In time, of course, the party evolved, and the constitution was altered; but the principle of popular government remained. It was not the invention of Button Gwinnett, but by espousing it as vigorously as he did, by rising as its champion, for whatever reason, he contributed much that was good and lasting to the revolutionary movement in Georgia. It was in this, one can easily see, that Lyman Hall was right: "Gwinnett [was], if possible a Whig to Excess."

A Note on Sources

The earliest study of Gwinnett was written by Hugh McCall and published in John Sanderson, ed., *Biography of the Signers of the Declaration of Independence,* V (Philadelphia, 1828) pp. 251-261. Other articles and sketches are Charles C. Jones, Jr., "Button Gwinnett," *Biographical Sketches of the Delegates from Georgia to the Continental Congress* (Boston, 1891), pp. 48-67; Walter G. Charlton, "Button Gwinnett (1732-1777)," *Georgia Historical Quarterly,* 8 (June 1924), 146-58; Roger A. Martin, "Button Gwinnett, 1735-1777," in Kenneth Coleman and Jackie Erney, eds., *Famous Georgians* (Atlanta, 1976), pp. 20-21; William J. Robertson, "Rare Button Gwinnett," *Georgia Historical Quarterly,* 30 (December 1946), 297-307; John D. Wade, "Button Gwinnett," *Dictionary of American Biography,* VIII (New York, 1932), pp. 56-66; plus a number of popular pieces in various magazines. Charles F. Jenkins, *Button Gwinnett, Signer of the Declaration of Independence* (New York, 1926), remains the only book on Gwinnett, though to produce a work of this length the author went into considerable detail on family origins, added an appendix of "known signatures," and included a number of pertinent documents. Factually, Jenkins' work is sound, but in trying to guarantee that "a greater measure of justice [would] be accorded the memory of Button Gwinnett" he cast his subject in a heroic mold which really did not do justice to his abilities as a practical politician. Despite this reservation Jenkins' study remains valuable in the understanding of Gwinnett and his career.

Apart from the documents reproduced in Jenkins' biography, primary material on Gwinnett is scarce and scattered. Because his career was so linked

58

with that of Lachlan McIntosh, a handy listing of manuscript collections and published sources relating to his activities can be found in the biography of the general cited below. Since that biography appeared, one additional collection with documents pertaining to the signer has come to the author's attention. The papers of Richard Waln, Jr., in the Historical Society of Pennsylvania, contain some indication of Gwinnett's post-England, pre-Georgia exploits. A general overview of what the Waln manuscripts reveal can be found in "Adventures of the Brigantine Rebecca: Wherein a Quaker Shipowner Becomes Involved With One B. Gwinnett," written by Joseph Carson and published in the *Autograph Collectors' Journal* (Fall 1952).

Parts of this sketch of Button Gwinnett have previously appeared in the following publications: Harvey H. Jackson, *Lachlan McIntosh and the Politics of Revolutionary Georgia* (Athens: The University of Georgia Press, 1979), ————————————, "Button Gwinnett and the Rise of the 'Western Members': A Reappraisal of Georgia's Whig to Excess'," *The Atlanta Historical Journal*, XXIV (2) (Summer 1980), 17-30;———, " 'Whig to Excess' or 'Scoundrell and Lying Rascal'? Just Who, or What Was Button Gwinnett," *American History Illustrated* (August 1981) and in the *Georgia Gazette*. The author wishes to thank the editors and publishers of these publications for granting permission to use this material. The author would like to thank Kathie Robichaud for reading a draft of this essay and making many excellent suggestions, and also Jerri Hager, Sara Palmer, and Sandra Rodgers for their help with the typing.

Chapter V

GEORGE WALTON

Edwin C. Bridges

F or years George Walton has been an enigma to those who have studied his career. He was twice governor of Georgia, a three-term chief justice of the state, a long-time delegate to the Continental Congress, and a signer of the Declaration of Independence. He was recognized by his fellow citizens as a "man of talent and merit" and "the patriot of '76." Georgia's first historian, Hugh McCall, knew Walton personally and wrote of him that Walton "always preserved, throughout his political career, the character of an honest, determined and perservering patriot." Robert Morris characterized him to George Washington as "a worthy man . . . a sound good lawyer and a very honest man."

These words of praise, however, do not tell the whole story of George Walton. "How greatly my dear Sir have you and I been deceived in the opinion we entertained of one Man whom we esteemed as a real patriot . . .? Can you believe that this wretch has a heart as callous, as adamant and to the last degree avaricious that he would sacrifice and destroy his best friends to accomplish any favorite point he had in view and in short that

Nero of infamous memory was not a greater Tyrant than G[eorge] W[alton]." Yet another critic wrote: "Aristocracy and arrogance, empty pride and presumptuousness, are his darling passions . . . and we have greatly to lament that a man, who in every respect answers this description, should be vested with the powers of judging and terminating on grievances by the laws of our country."

For the province and then the state of Georgia, the last three decades of the eighteenth century were years of remarkable upheaval and growth. Throughout this entire period, George Walton was at or near the center stage of politics. Despite his prominence, however, Walton has somehow remained enshrouded in mystery and controversy. At one moment he appeared a solid member of one political camp, only to emerge a short time later as the leader of another. His apparent inconsistency and opportunism — and the enraged reaction of many of his contemporary opponents — have intrigued and perplexed generations of Georgia historians. Yet, when Walton's life is seen as a whole, a consistency of interests, style, and philosophy can be found that helps make sense of the confusing turns of his career.

In September 1749, thirty-two-year-old Robert Walton of Goochland County, Virginia, added a codicil to his will. The change provided for a young daughter and for "the child my wife now goes with." Nine months later, on June 25, 1750, Robert Walton's widow, Mary Hughes Walton, appeared in the court of Cumberland County, Virginia, to prove the will of her deceased husband. Between September 1749 and the following June, Robert Walton had died. During the same period, his son George was born.

Mrs. Walton did not survive her husband by many years. By the time he was seven years old, their son was an orphan under the guardianship of his father's brother — also named George Walton — who had recently married Martha Hughes, the sister of (the younger Walton's mother) Mary Hughes Walton, Many

Walton's life describe his childhood as a particularly unhappy one, a tradition which is difficult to deny or to confirm. His uncle was a man of relatively ample means, but George and Marth Walton had thirteen children of their own to rear, in addition to those of their deceased brother and sister.

In 1765, the fifteen-year-old George Walton apprenticed himself to a builder, Christopher Ford, to be taught the "Art of House Carpenter and Joiner." Before he finished his term of apprenticeship, however, Walton secured a release from the indenture; and in 1769, at the age of nineteen, he traveled to Savannah, Georgia, where he prepared to begin again in a new occupation. One of Walton's older brothers, John, had moved to Augusta several years earlier and had quickly established himself as a planter, merchant, and surveyor. Probably with his brother's help, Walton secured a position as clerk in the office of Savannah attorney Henry Yonge, Jr. By January 1770, he was witnessing legal papers for Yonge — the first signed records documenting Walton's arrival in Savannah. By 1772, he had received sufficient training in law to pay the £2/14 "fee of admittance" allowing him to appear before the Georgia general court.

The chief justice of the court, Anthony Stokes, kept a careful record of the fees he received. Except for Walton and another beginner, all the attorneys Stokes listed in 1772 were identified by the title "Esquire." Walton was recorded merely as "Mr. George Walton, Attorney at Law." He was the seventh of nine attorneys in a list ranked by the total fees paid. Walton had paid £11 for the year compared to £111 paid by the most active attorney, John Houstoun.

By January 1774, signs of Walton's success began to appear. That month, Governor James Wright commissioned "George Walton, Gentleman" as lieutenant of the Eighth Company of the First Georgia Regiment of militia. Meanwhile, Walton's law practice had also begun to prosper. By 1775, only three years after his first appearance in court, he had more litigation before Chief Justice Stokes than any other attorney in the province. In the January term alone, he paid £80 in fees, and, in the April term, the total soared to £140 — more than most attorneys paid in the course of an entire year. In six years Walton had risen from carpenter's apprentice to the position of a prosperous attorney, and, in form at least, he was regarded as a "gentleman" by the governing authorities of the province.

Walton's rapid professional growth coincided with the growth of American opposition to the policies of Great Britain. This opposition was slow in taking root in Georgia compared with its pace in colonies to the north, and local expressions of discontent were cautious and tentative. Nevertheless two centers of provincial protests were clearly identifiable by 1774. St. John's Parish, an area dominated by congregationalist transplants from New England, was the more aggressive. The other was Savannah, where a group of young men, many of them the scions of the province's leading families, began to voice their opinions. As a relative newcomer to Savannah, Walton did not enjoy the social prestige of many of his colleagues; but his skill and energy earned him a position of leadership in the ranks of these young Whigs.

These two different centers of revolutionary activity are an indication of the debilitating lack of cohesion that characterized Georgia society and politics in the late-eighteenth century. In a province as young as Georgia, with so many differing interest groups, the Loyalists might well have retained their dominance had there not been support from other colonies for the Georgia protest effort. Not until fighting actually began in Massachusetts did the various Whig factions finally unite; and not until late 1775 and early 1776 did they completely wrest control of the provincial government from the royal authorities.

As a resident of Savannah, Walton enjoyed the acceptance of many of the merchants and planters there; but he also had connections with other elements of Georgia society. His two brothers and other Virginia neighbors and relatives had settled, not in Savannah, but in the Georgia backcountry in and around Augusta. The fact that Walton was from the Virginia backcountry and was related to or acquainted with many settlers in the Georgia backcountry allowed him to represent the views of both that section and of the coastal area where he lived. His energy, legal skill, and personal attractiveness had already been demonstrated in his successful law practice. He was a natural choice in elections requiring a compromise between Savannah and the backcountry.

The pace of Walton's success in Georgia's revolutionary politics reflected these advantages. He was elected secretary of the provincial congress in July 1775 and then president of the Council of Safety the following December. He was also one of the ranking officers in the state militia, and, in early 1776, he was chosen as one of the Georgia representatives to the Continental Congress. Because of delays in leaving Georgia and illness as he traveled, Walton did not arrive in Philadelphia until late June — literally hours before the most celebrated event in American history.

George Walton's first appearance was not noted in the congressional journals because Lyman Hall and Button Gwinnett had already presented the credentials for the Georgia delegation. According to his own later statements, he was present in the Congress on July 1 — the last day Congress met as a committee of the whole to consider the question of declaring independence. Although the issue had already been thoroughly discussed, John Dickenson of Pennsylvania concluded the debate with a formal summary of the arguments against a declaration. New delegates arrived from New Jersey and asked for a response to Dickenson and a recapitulation of the reasons for a declaration. In the silence following this request, the eyes of Congress turned toward John Adams, who gratified his colleagues with a speech that lived on in the memory of many who were present that day. Almost 15 years later Walton wrote to Adams recalling his impressions: "Since the first day of July, 1776, my conduct, in every station in life, has corresponded with the result of that great question which you so ably and faithfully developed on that day. . . . It was then I felt the strongest attachments and they have never departed from me." After many hours of additional work on the precise wording, the Declaration of Independence was finally approved on July 4. The formal signing of the engrossed copy did not take place until August 2.

Benjamin Rush, a prominent Philadelphia physician who was a member of Congress, later recorded his impressions of his fellow delegates. Of Walton, he wrote: "A sensible young man. He possessed knowledge and a pleasing manner of speaking. He was the youngest member of congress[,] being not quite three and twenty when he signed the Declaration of Independence." Actually Walton was 26; but he was still apparently the youngest of the signers.

Walton served four one-year terms in the Congress, 1776-'77 and 1780-'81. Although his record was not brilliant, he participated in important elements of the Congress's work, such as service on the Marine Committee, on the 1776-'77 Executive Committee, and on lesser committees appointed to consider Indian relations, prisoner of war problems, and numerous individual petitions. In national political matters Walton usually joined with the conservative Virginia and mid-Atlantic delegates against the more radical New Englanders and their allies. His most significant contributions grew out of his efforts to secure assistance for Georgia. He spent substantial portions of his time trying to impress his colleagues with Georgia's strategic importance, maneuvering to obtain additional funds, troops, and supplies for the state, and handling constituent services — particularly the requests of Georgians who were suffering in some way because of the war.

Because of his critical position in the flow of information and power, Walton was inevitably (and not unwillingly) drawn into the factional contests that soon began to resurface among Georgia Whigs. The coalition that had been formed to drive out the royal authorities was too fragile to survive after its goal was attained. With the displacement of traditional leaders, no single group was able to establish a dominant position. Each contending faction began to press its particular interests, and ambitious local leaders wore the colors of those interests as they tried to assert their personal claims for provincial leadership. For the entire war, Georgia politics was characterized by the frustrated efforts of the Whigs to build a unified government and by the continued struggles of contentious factions and leaders to gain dominance. Walton joined in this struggle from his position in Congress, working energetically to advance the fortunes of his friends and to torpedo those of his enemies.

After serving in Congress sixteen months, Walton returned to Savannah in late 1777. He reported to friends in Philadelphia that during this time he was trying to limit his political involvement and to take care of his personal affairs. He resumed his legal practice, purchased a home in Savannah, and married thirteen-year-old Dorothy Camber. She was the daughter of Thomas Camber of St. Peter's Parish, South Carolina, who had died a few years earlier, and of Dorothy Butler Camber of Chatham County.

Despite the importance of these personal matters, Walton could not remain aloof from the political and military conflicts swirling about him. He rejoined the Georgia Assembly, which he was entitled to do as one of the state's congressional delegates; and, in November 1778, he also served with the militia trying to repel an attack by the British from Florida. In late December, only four months after Walton's wedding, the British launched a major invasion of Georgia at Savannah. As the British landed their forces and arranged them in formation against Major General Robert Howe's defenders, Walton became aware of a serious weakness in the American right flank. If the British learned of a pathway through the swamp, they could easily outflank the American position. After informing Howe of his concern, Walton ordered his 100-man militia unit toward this unprotected area; but as they arrived the British regulars were just emerging from the pathway and drawing up in attack formation. After a brief, unsuccessful attempt to hold their ground, Walton's men and General Howe's entire command fled in retreat. Walton was gravely wounded and captured, and spent the next ten months as a prisoner of war in Savannah and then at Sunbury.

Walton was not formally released from his oath as a prisoner of war until an exchange following the unsuccessful Franco-American seige of Savannah in October 1779. Immediately after his release, the new commander of the American forces in the South, General Benjamin Lincoln, urged Walton to visit the Georgia backcountry to reassure the people there of Lincoln's continued concern for their safety. Although a provisional council had been set up earlier in Augusta by John Wereat to help carry on state duties, it was not a constitutionally-formed government, and Lincoln also urged Walton to help correct this deficiency. Interpreting this request as a mandate to establish a new constitutional government, Walton energetically undertook the task.

The Walton government of 1779 marks one of the perplexing turns in his career. The people with whom he now began to work were the old supporters of Button Gwinnett — members of the faction Walton had previously opposed while he was in Congress. In fact, Walton had been instrumental in having Lachlan McIntosh appointed, instead of Gwinnett, to command the continental army in Georgia. Walton was also responsible for John Wereat's appointment as the agent for the powerful Marine Committee of the Continental Congress. Now, in 1779, Walton opposed his former friends and allied himself with his former opponents. The government he thus helped launch returned the favor by selecting him governor, and their alliance was sealed by the adoption of a broad slate of measures favored by the

GEORGE WALTON

backcountry — the constituency from which this new coalition drew its support. The Assembly liberalized requirements for land grants, expanded the dragoons, and flirted with the idea of a new military campaign against the Indians. One other important action was a request sent to Congress, bearing the signature of the speaker of the house, calling for the removal of Lachlan McIntosh from his command in Georgia.

After the war, Walton wrote to Benjamin Rush that he had gathered all his papers together to write a defense of his actions. Unfortunately neither the defense nor his papers have survived. We are left only with conjectures and the scattered comments of other observers — many of whom were Walton's opponents. One explanation that has been offered for Walton's change of political allegiances is that he learned during his captivity of the great injury being inflicted on the American cause by Tory sympathizers — some of whom were close friends of McIntosh. A related explanation concerns the continuing controversy in Georgia over control of the continental brigade — a clash in which Walton advocated state civilian control and McIntosh opposed it.

There are so many elements of convenience in Walton's change that it is hard to ignore them also as factors. When Walton first reached Augusta in late October 1779, most of the old conservative Whigs had fled the state. He may have then begun working with the radicals who remained — Richard Howly and George Wells — and he may have found them to be acceptable allies. When some of the conservatives began to return, he may not have wanted this new arrangement changed. The radicals were politically stronger than the conservatives, as evidenced by the elections for the 1780 Assembly; Walton may have recognized and acquiesced to this political strength. Also, the Wereat government of 1779 having failed to reappoint him to Congress, he may have resented this omission and turned to others who would support him.

One additional factor was money. By assuring General

Lincoln that a new constitutional government was formed, Walton expected that the state could finally receive money that the Congress had authorized. Lincoln had not released the money to Wereat's council because it was not a constitutional body. Another financial consideration related to a difference in philosophy over the payment of state officials. The conservatives felt that government service was a social obligation for those who were fit to govern and who could afford to serve without the expectation of financial reward. The radicals, however, felt that public officers had to be financially supported at a level consistent with the authority they represented. Men, like George Walton, with limited resources might not have been able to serve unless they received support from the government.

Just over a month after his election as governor, Walton was selected again to represent Georgia in the Continental Congress. He left the state in late January 1781 and resumed his duties in Congress later that spring. The outcome of Walton's two years back in Georgia — with his election as governor and then his return to Congress — appeared to add yet another link to his chain of successes. This time, however, the tough factional infighting of Georgia politics caught up with him. His continued efforts to manipulate and influence the course of state political affairs had ended in excesses and would result in his humiliation.

William Glascock, the speaker of the house whose name had appeared on the letter requesting McIntosh's removal, wrote to Congress in the spring of 1780 that the letter had been sent without his consent or even his knowledge — that it was a forgery. Lachlan McIntosh himself worked aggressively to clear his name and eventually went to Philadelphia to present his case in person. The best defense Walton could offer was that during the difficult time of his governorship public affairs were too disrupted for every action to have been taken in perfect form. He continued to assert that his government's criticism of McIntosh reflected the general will of the people. Despite these arguments, Congress repudiated its dismissal of McIntosh and restored him to his original rank. Back in Georgia, the state Assembly compounded Walton's humiliation by defeating his absentee bid for a new term in Congress.

Despite the fact that he had lost his seat in Congress, Walton and his family remained in Philadelphia from the fall of 1781 until late 1782, after the British had evacuated Savannah. When he finally did return in the winter of 1782-'83, he was welcomed by a broadside volley that McIntosh and his angry allies had long been preparing: a legislative investigation, a published series of critical letters, a horsewhipping at the hands of McIntosh's son, and an effort to prosecute him for forgery. A committee appointed by the state legislature to consider the charges against Walton heard substantial evidence in January 1783 of his culpability. The day before the committee was to make its report, however, the Assembly itself voted on the appointment of the new chief justice of Georgia for the coming year. Their choice — an astounding one under the circumstances — was George Walton. Despite the fierceness of attacks against him, Walton served three one-year terms as chief justice until, tired by the rigors of the long circuit rides, he apparently decided of his own volition to relinquish the office.

Even though Walton was victorious over McIntosh, the post-war years were extremely difficult ones for him. He remained subject to the suspicion and criticism of many of his colleagues, and he also suffered severe financial reversals. He tried unsuccessfully to establish himself near Savannah as a rice planter, and he also speculated moderately but without notable success in land. By 1787, his financial position had deteriorated so badly that he began disposing of his Savannah property and moved to the interior part of the state near Augusta, where his two older brothers and other members of his family had settled.

This move, apparently dictated by personal necessity, was quickly blessed by the fortunes of politics. Walton was elected governor of Georgia again in 1789. His second administration attempted to deal with those ongoing concerns that preoccupied most politically active Georgians during the post-war years: the closely connected issues of Indian relations, westward expansion, and the relationship between state and federal government. Walton had long been one of Georgia's most ardent supporters of a strengthened national government, and he continued this support through the state's unanimous ratification of the federal Constitution. During his administration a new state constitution was also written and approved to bring the state into closer harmony with the new national government. Like most Georgians, Walton favored a strong defense against the Indians and the acquisition of additional Indian land for new settlement. At the same time, he advocated control and moderation by Georgia citizens so that relations with the Indians would be peaceful and new territorial acquisitions could be secured and settled in a fair and orderly manner.

In one important area of public policy Governor Walton allowed the start of a practice that brought national discredit upon the state. Since the end of the trustee period Georgia had followed a liberal policy in dispensing public lands so that immigration would be encouraged. After the war, generous bounties were offered so that virtually anyone who was not proven a Tory was eligible for land — many under several different types of bounty arrangements. A further liberalization measure decentralized the application process so that determinations of eligibility could be handled by county land courts instead of by state officials. During Walton's term as governor, a county land court approved and sent for his signature sets of plats and warrants that covered enormous tracts of land and that were obviously fraudulent. Arguing that he was bound to sign all grant applications approved by county courts unless formal caveats were entered against them, Walton affixed his signature and gave the fraudulent grants the appearance of authenticity. Land speculation had been a problem since the war; but this precedent allowed a new and more vicious round of fraud to begin — a scandal which came to be known as the "pine barren speculation." Walton's legal reasons for this position of "executive restraint" may have been correct, but his motives appear to have been clouded by his close friendship with Robert Morris, one of the major sellers of these fraudulent grants. Several years later, Walton provided the salesmen for those tracts with his personal deposition proclaiming the desirability and productivity of the pine barren lands.

At the end of his term as governor, Walton expressed to his friends his desire to continue in public service in the judicial department. He tried to use his old contacts to persuade President Washington to appoint him to the Supreme Court or to a federal district judgeship. Washington, who had been a friend of Lachlan McIntosh, ignored Walton's requests and the letters of Walton's friends. The 1789 Georgia Constitution divided the old position of chief justice into two district superior court judgeships. Walton's friends in Georgia were more responsive to his desires than was President Washington, and Walton was selected by the state legislature as one of the new superior court judges.

During the early 1790s, a new scheme of land speculation — on a far greater scale than the pine barrens — began to take hold in Georgia. After an unsuccessful series of efforts to establish settlements on Indian land in the 1780s, the state legislature approved the sale to three land companies of several large tracts of western land (substantial portions of present-day Alabama and Mississippi). This first Yazoo sale fell through because of the inability of the companies to make their payments quickly in specie. That unsuccessful effort whetted the appetite of the land companies, and they soon launched a new, more extensive scheme, part of which involved securing the support of public officials or replacing those who were obdurate with supporters committed to the sale. Walton initially denounced these efforts, an action that reportedly caused him to lose his bid for re-election as judge because of the land companies' opposition. Later, however, he appears to have reached some type of accommodation with the speculators. He was reported to own a share in one of the Yazoo companies, and several of his close friends and relatives were also involved in the purchase. Walton was again elected judge in 1794; and, after the Yazoo act was passed in early 1795, he defended it in his charges to county grand juries.

Georgians, such as Walton, who supported the sale were shocked at the intensity and bitterness of the public reaction against it. When James Jackson resigned his U.S. Senate seat to return home and lead a repeal effort, his cause became a crusade that swept aside every opponent who tried to stand and fight. Walton was appointed to fill Jackson's unexpired Senate term, and he was able to weather part of the storm in Philadelphia. He was not elected to the Senate for a term in his own right, however, undoubtedly because of his association with the Yazoo land sale. He returned to Georgia in mid-1796. Reluctant to oppose Jackson openly on the Yazoo issue, Walton and his colleagues responded with a kind of political guerrilla war, attacking him for his support of the French, for his failure to support President Adams, and also for what they claimed to be Jackson's dictatorial practices in Georgia. Their efforts bore some fruit, and Walton was again returned to the office of superior court judge, despite Jackson's energetic opposition.

Walton was still active in his last years, but the activity lacked the scope and impact of his earlier career. He was involved in efforts to establish and locate a state university, as well as in other local concerns. Although he was hampered increasingly by illnesses, he continued to serve as a superior court judge and to speak out vigorously on public matters of importance. Walton died in February 1804, only two months after the death of his oldest son, whom he had loved dearly.

In the last chaotic quarter of the eighteenth century, few Georgians could match Walton's record for variety,

"MEADOW GARDEN,"
HOME OF GEORGE WALTON, IN AUGUSTA
This 1901 photograph was made after the house had been
restored by the Georgia Society, Daughters of the American
Revolution.

controversy, and political success. He was blessed with personal attributes of charm, skill, and tenacity; but his success also derived from the mix of his political beliefs, which was, if not totally unique, at least unusual. He was able to count himself among the most radical of Georgians in his desire to purge Loyalists, his determination to continue the war at any cost, and his efforts to remain free of British economic influence after the war. In state-federal relations, Walton was an outspoken advocate of increased power for the Congress — a position many southerners strongly opposed. Although he enjoyed substantial support from western Georgia and energetically advocated measures of interest to that area, he made no effort to project himself as a democrat. In fact, he consistently supported measures to strengthen the government, to support its authority and dignity, and to restore order and social control to Georgia society. In his personal life, he attempted to live the life of a gentleman and to carry himself in a manner he thought befitted his distinguished station.

This unique blending of conservative and radical elements, like Walton's unique combination of personal connections, allowed him considerable flexibility in shaping his position according to what he thought best for his state and, critics said, for himself. His apparent opportunism has raised the critical brows of many Georgia historians and has prompted charges that cannot be totally denied. At the same time an overall view of his career reveals a reasonable pattern of consistency from the perspective of the unusual general philosophy he espoused. Walton himself professed a sincere desire to do what was best for the state; and, despite the aura of controversy that enveloped him through most of his career, many of his contemporaries accepted this profession.

A Note on Sources

This chapter is based on the author's dissertation, "George Walton: A Political Biography" (University of Chicago, 1981). The issues discussed here are addressed more fully and are documented in that work. Because of his wide-ranging career and also the popularity of documents written by signers of the Declaration of Independence, historical information about Walton has been scattered in an almost unimaginable variety of locations. Walton manuscripts have been found in approximately thirty institutions — from the British Public Record Office to the Maine Historical Society to the James S. Copley Library in La Jolla, California. Sources of various official documents are equally rich, though not so numerous or so geographically dispersed. The papers of the Continental Congress in the National Archives and the records of the state and local governments at the Georgia Department of Archives and History provide a great deal of information about Walton's public life. Various series of published documents also provide important source material — such as *Collections of the Georgia Historical Society, Letters of the Members of the Continental Congress,* and *American State Papers.* The revolutionary and early national periods of Georgia history have attracted the attention of a number of excellent scholars during the past ten years. The author has the good fortune to count many of these people as personal friends. He has enjoyed and profited from their insights both through their published works and through personal discussion. Those who have contributed particularly to this work are Edward J. Cashin, Kenneth Coleman, Harold E. Davis, Robert S. Davis, Harvey H. Jackson, George R. Lamplugh, Virginia Redd, Heard Robertson, Gordon Smith, Paul Smith, and Kenneth H. Thomas, Jr.

IN CONGRESS. JULY 4, 1776.

The unanimous Declaration of the thirteen united States of America.

THE DECLARATION OF INDEPENDENCE

On permanent display in the National Archives, Washington, D.C.

Chapter VI

THE DECLARATION OF INDEPENDENCE

In Congress, July 4, 1776

THE UNANIMOUS DECLARATION OF THE THIRTEEN UNITED STATES OF AMERICA,

When in the Course of human events, it becomes necessary for one people to dissolve the political bands which have connected them with another, and to assume among the Powers of the earth, the separate and equal station to which the Laws of Nature and of Nature's God entitle them, a decent respect to the opinions of mankind requires that they should declare the causes which impel them to the separation.

We hold these truths to be self-evident, that all men are created equal, that they are endowed by their Creator with certain unalienable Rights, that among these are Life, Liberty and the pursuit of Happiness. That to secure these rights, Governments are instituted among Men, deriving their just powers from the consent of the governed, That whenever any Form of Government becomes destructive of these ends, it is the Right of the People to alter or to abolish it, and to institute new Government, laying its foundation on such principles and organizing its powers in such form, as to them shall seem most likely to effect their Safety and Happiness. Prudence, indeed, will dictate that Governments long established should not be changed for light and transient causes; and accordingly all experience hath shown, that mankind are more disposed to suffer, while evils are sufferable, than to right themselves by abolishing the forms to which they are accustomed. But when a long train of abuses and usurpations, pursuing invariably the same Objective evinces a design to reduce them under absolute Despotism, it is their right, it is their duty, to throw off such Government, and to provide new Guards for their future security.— Such has been the patient sufferance of these Colonies; and such is now the necessity which constrains them to alter their former Systems of Government. The history of the present King of Great Britain is a history of repeated injuries and usurpations, all having in direct object the establishment of an absolute Tyranny over these States. To prove this, let Facts be submitted to a candid world.

He has refused his Assent to Laws, the most wholesome and necessary for the public good.

He has forbidden his Governors to pass Laws of immediate and pressing importance, unless suspended in their operation till his Assent should be obtained; and when so suspended, he has utterly neglected to attend to them.

He has refused to pass other Laws for the accommodation of large districts of people, unless those people would relinquish the right of Representation in the Legislature, a right inestimable to them and formidable to tyrants only.

He has called together legislative bodies at places unusual, uncomfortable, and distant from the depository of their Public Records, for the sole purpose of fatiguing them into compliance with his measures.

He has dissolved Representative Houses repeatedly, for opposing with manly firmness his invasions on the rights of the people.

He has refused for a long time, after such dissolutions, to cause others to be elected; whereby the Legislative Powers, incapable of Annihilation, have returned to the People at large for their exercise; the State remaining in the mean time exposed to all the dangers of invasion from without, and convulsions within.

He has endeavoured to prevent the population of these States; for that purpose obstructing the Laws of Naturalization of Foreigners; refusing to pass others to encourage their migration hither, and raising the conditions of new Appropriations of Lands.

He has obstructed the Administration of Justice, by refusing his Assent to Laws for establishing Judiciary Powers.

He has made Judges dependent on his Will alone, for the tenure of their offices, and the amount and payment of their salaries.

He has erected a multitude of New Offices, and sent hither swarms of Officers to harass our People, and eat out their substance.

He has kept among us, in times of peace, Standing Armies without the Consent of our legislature.

He has affected to render the Military independent of and superior to the Civil Power.

He has combined with others to subject us to a jurisdiction foreign to our constitution, and unacknowledged by our laws; giving his Assent to their acts of pretended legislation:

For quartering large bodies of armed troops among us:

For protecting them, by a mock Trial, from Punishment for any Murders which they should commit on the Inhabitants of these States:

For cutting off our Trade with all parts of the world:

For imposing taxes on us without our Consent:

For depriving us in many cases, of the benefits of Trial by Jury:

For transporting us beyond Seas to be tried for pretended offences:

For abolishing the free System of English Laws in a neighboring Province, establishing therein an Arbitrary government, and enlarging its Boundaries so as to render it at once an example and fit instrument for introducing the same absolute rule into these Colonies:

For taking away our Charters, abolishing our most valuable Laws, and altering fundamentally the Forms of our Governments:

For suspending our own Legislature, and declaring themselves invested with Power to legislate for us in all cases whatsoever.

He has abdicated Government here, by declaring us out of his Protection and waging War against us.

He has plundered our seas, ravaged our Coasts, burnt our towns, and destroyed the lives of our people.

He is at this time transporting large armies of foreign mercenaries to compleat the works of death, desolation and tyranny, already begun with circumstances of Cruelty & perfidy scarcely paralleled in the most barbarous ages, and totally unworthy the Head of a civilized nation.

He has constrained our fellow Citizens taken Captive on the high Seas to bear Arms against their Country, to become the executioners of their friends and Brethren, or to fall themselves by their Hands.

He has excited domestic insurrections amongst us, and has endeavoured to bring on the inhabitants of our frontiers, the merciless Indian Savages, whose known rule of warfare, is an undistinguished destruction of all ages, sexes and conditions.

In every stage of these Oppressions We have Petitioned for Redress in the most humble terms: Our repeated Petitions have been answered only by repeated injury. A Prince, whose character is thus marked by every act which may define a Tyrant, is unfit to be the ruler of a free People.

Nor have We been wanting in attention to our British brethren. We have warned them from time to time of attempts by their legislature to extend an unwarrantable jurisdiction over us. We have reminded them of the circumstances of our emigration and settlement here. We have appealed to their native justice and magnanimity, and we have conjured them to the ties of our common kindred to disavow these usurpations,

**GEORGIA'S DELEGATES
SIGN THE DECLARATION**
Left to right: Button Gwinnett, George Walton, and Lyman Hall

which would inevitably interrupt our connections and correspondence. They too have been deaf to the voice of justice and of consanguinity. We must, therefore, acquiesce in the necessity, which denounces our Separation, and hold them, as we hold the rest of mankind, Enemies in War, in Peace Friends.

We, therefore, the Representatives of the United States of America, in General Congress, Assembled, appealing to the Supreme Judge of the world for the rectitude of our intentions, do, in the Name, and by Authority of the good People of these Colonies, solemnly publish and declare, That these United Colonies are, and of Right ought to be Free and Independent States; that they are Absolved from all Allegiance to the British Crown, and that all political connection between them and the State of Great Britian, is and ought to be totally dissolved; and that as Free and Independent States, they have full Power to levy War, conclude Peace, contract Alliances, establish Commerce, and to do all other Acts and Things which Independent States may of right do. And for the support of this Declaration, with a firm reliance on the Protection of Divine Providence, we mutually pledge to each other our Lives, our Fortunes and our sacred Honor.

JOHN HANCOCK.

[Georgia]
BUTTON GWINNETT,
LYMAN HALL,
GEO. WALTON.

[North Carolina]
WM. HOOPER,
JOSEPH HEWES,
JOHN PENN.

[South Carolina]
EDWARD RUTLEDGE,
THOS. HEYWARD, JUNR.,
THOMAS LYNCH, JUNR.,
ARTHUR MIDDLETON.

[*Maryland*]
SAMUEL CHASE,
WM. PACA,
THOS. STONE,
CHARLES CARROLL OF CARROLLTON.

[*Virginia*]
GEORGE WYTHE,
RICHARD HENRY LEE,
TH. JEFFERSON,
BENJA. HARRISON,
THS. NELSON, JR.,
FRANCIS LIGHTFOOT LEE,
CARTER BRAXTON.

[*Delaware*]
CAESAR RODNEY,
GEO. READ,
THO. M'KEAN.

[*New Jersey*]
RICHD. STOCKTON,
JNO. WITHERSPOON,
FRAS. HOPKINSON,
JOHN HART,
ABRA. CLARK.

[*Pennsylvania*]
ROBT. MORRIS,
BENJAMIN RUSH,
BENJA. FRANKLIN,
JOHN MORTON,
GEO. CLYMER,
JAS. SMITH,
GEO. TAYLOR,
JAMES WILSON,
GEO. ROSS.

[*New York*]
WM. FLOYD,
PHIL. LIVINGSTON,
FRANS. LEWIS,
LEWIS MORRIS.

[*New Hampshire*]
JOSIAH BARTLETT,
WM. WHIPPLE,
MATTHEW THORNTON.

[*Massachusetts-Bay*]
SAML. ADAMS,
JOHN ADAMS,
ROBT. TREAT PAINE,
ELBRIDGE GERRY.

[*Rhode Island*]
STEP. HOPKINS,
WILLIAM ELLERY.

[*Connecticut*]
ROGER SHERMAN,
SAM'EL HUNTINGTON,
WM. WILLIAMS,
OLIVER WOLCOTT.

Chapter VII

GENEALOGIES OF THE SIGNERS

Kenneth H. Thomas, Jr.

LYMAN HALL came to Georgia via South Carolina from Connecticut, where he was born in Wallingford on April 12, 1724. As the fifth child, and third son, of John (d. 1773, age 80) and Mary Street Hall (d. 1778, age 81), who had married in 1716, and grandson of John and Mary Lyman Hall, all of the same community, he grew up in the Puritan environment of his New England ancestors.

Hall's brothers and sisters were remembered in 1870 to have been Hannah, born 1717; John, died 1737; Eunice (married Dr. John Dickinson of Middletown, Conn.); Street (1721-1809), left descendants in Wallingford; Susannah, born 1726 (married Elisha Whittelsey); Giles (1733-1789), left descendants in Wallingford; Rhoda (1734-1751); and Mary (m. Mr. Foote).

In 1769, Lyman Hall purchased a plantation near Midway Church that became known as "Hall's Knoll," the site of which was marked in 1954 by a Georgia Historical Marker placed on U.S. 17, one mile north of the church in present-day Liberty County, Georgia.

On May 12, 1790, the Halls sold this property, which had been developed as a rice and indigo plantation, and moved to "Montville," at Shell Bluff, on the Savannah River in Burke County, Georgia. The deeds were lost in fires at the Burke County Courthouse.

Lyman Hall, "late Governor," died at the age of 67 on October 19, 1790, at his plantation in Burke County.

Hall's grave remained intact until 1848, when his remains were reinterred under the Signers' Monument in Augusta along with those of George Walton. The original marble tombstone was sent to his birthplace, where it was dedicated July 5, 1858. It remains today at Center Street Burying Ground.

Lyman Hall married (1) in Fairfield, Connecticut, on May 20, 1752, Abigail Burr, a daughter of Thaddus and Abigail Sturges Burr. She died July 8, 1753, without issue, and is buried at Fairfield's Old Burying Ground.

Hall married (2) (date unknown) Mary Osborne, born August 8, 1736, daughter of Samuel and Hannah Osborne of Fairfield. Her ancestry is discussed in *History and Genealogy of the Families of Old Fairfield* (1930), by Donald L. Jacobus. Having survived both Dr. Hall and their only child, she died "at her plantation in Burke County" on November 18, 1793, and is in an unmarked grave near her son.

Although the records of Dr. Hall's estate were lost in a Burke County Courthouse fire, his widow's will was copied and is found in *Genealogical Notes: Relating to the Families of Hon. Lyman Hall of Georgia. . .*(Albany, N.Y., 1886), by Theodore Parsons Hall. The copy was furnished that author by C.C. Jones, Jr., of Augusta, Georgia, a noted historian.

Lyman and Mary Hall had only one child:

John, born in Charleston, December 4, 1765, who died without issue "at his plantation in Burke County" at the age of 26 on January 20, 1792. With his death, the direct line of Lyman Hall ended. His tomb remains on the plantation where the gravesite of the Lyman Hall family was marked by the National Society, Daughters of the American Revolution in 1936 and by a Georgia

Historical Marker in 1958. It is located off Georgia 56 at McBean's Creek, near the Burke-Richmond County line on the Savannah River.

A biography is *Lyman Hall: Georgia Patriot,* published in 1959 by James William Hall, a 1951 graduate of the University of North Carolina, now an attorney in Valdosta, Georgia.

A recent honor bestowed on Dr. Lyman Hall was the dedication on December 13, 1975, of a marker in his memory at the Midway Church.

Other Hall lines — There are many Hall families that share either kinship or a common name with the signer.

Lyman Hall (1859-1905), second president of Georgia Tech, was a native of Americus, a son of John E. Hall and an 1881 graduate of the United States Military Academy. He married in 1883 Anne Toombs Jennings of Charleston, South Carolina, and had four children, the sons being Stovall Hall and R.B. Hall.

Lyman Hall (1826-1903) married Elizabeth Durden (1830-1906) and had thirteen children. They are buried at Gadara Church Cemetery, McCrae, Florida. Merrill E. Glisson of Keystone Heights, Florida, is a grandson.

The descendants of Hugh Moss Comer (1853-1934) of Savannah and his second wife, Lilla Coe Hall (b. 1853), of Wallingford, Connecticut, descend from Dr. Lyman Hall's grandfather John Hall (1670-1730). Among these are: Mary Comer Lane (Mrs. Howard) Morrison (b. 1907); Remer Young Lane, married Louise Harris; Mills Bee Lane, Jr., married Ann Waring; Lilla Train (Mrs. Samuel L.) Varnedoe; and Mary Anne Train (Mrs. Lawton M.) Calhoun, all of Savannah.

BUTTON GWINNETT was baptized April 10, 1735, in St. Catherine's Church, Gloucester, England. He died May 19, 1777, in Savannah, Georgia. He was a son of the Rev. Samuel Gwinnett (d. Aug. 13, 1777; buried at Down Hatherley, Gloucestershire), vicar there for fifty years of St. Mary's Church. His mother was Anne Emes of Twining (perhaps a widow; d. Aug. 16, 1767; buried at Down Hatherley), who had married the Rev. Mr. Gwinnett in 1727. She was related to the Prices and Buttons, hence her son's name. Button Gwinnett was the third of their seven known children:

1. Anna Maria, baptized March 11, 1731. Died February 7, 1745; buried at St. Nicholas Church in the village of St. Nicholas near the home known as "Cottrell" in Glamorganshire, Wales.

2. Samuel, Jr., baptized June 6, 1732. Died c. 1792 at "Cottrell." Married 1755 his cousin Emilia Button (d. 1785), after whose death he remained at "Cottrell," which had been her inheritance. At his death, it passed to his sister Emilia.

3. Button. More further.

4. Thomas Price, baptized November 1, 1736. Died young.

5. Robert, baptized August 22, 1738. Died young.

6. Emilia, baptized December 23, 1741. Died September 30, 1807. Buried at Newick, Sussex, probably at St. Mary's Church alongside her friend and benefactress, Lady Louise Vernon.

In 1786, Emilia inherited Penllyn Castle (also spelled Penllyne, Penlline) as a life estate under the will of Lady Louise Vernon. In 1792, she inherited "Cottrell" from her brother Samuel. Lady Vernon (1733-1786) was the only child of Bussy, Lord Mansell (d. 1750) and his second wife, Barbara Villiers. She married George Venables, who became, in 1780, Baron Vernon of Kenderton. She died childless and left her estates to friends rather than to her husband. "Newick Place," her home in Newick, Sussex, was left to the Dowager Lady Fortescue. Newick is north of Lewes, which is ten miles north of Brighton. Penllyn Castle and "Cottrell" are located between Cardiff and Bridgeend, Wales, near the town of Cowbridge. "Cottrell" is near the village of St. Nicholas, approximately six miles east of Cowbridge. Penllyn Castle is one and one-half miles west of Cowbridge, about five miles from Bridgeend.

After Emilia inherited Penllyn Castle, she built a mansion there. At her death, both it and "Cottrell" passed as life estates to

GRAVE OF BUTTON GWINNETT
Colonial Cemetery, Savannah

a first cousin of Lady Vernon, the second Earl of Clarendon, Thomas Villiers (1753-1824). By the 1840s, both were owned by Captain Sir George Tyler, Royal Navy (1792-1862).

   7. John Price. Died 1777. No issue known.

Button Gwinnett married April 19, 1757, in the Ancient Collegiate Church of Wolverhampton, Staffordshire, Anne Bourne, who was baptized there April 19, 1735. She was a daughter of Aaron Bourne, who married in 1732 Sarah Salt of Brewood, Staffordshire, a village six miles northwest of Wolverhampton.

Button and Ann Gwinnett had three daughters, all baptized in Wolverhampton:

   1. Amelia, baptized February 27, 1758. Died young.
   2. Ann, baptized May 14, 1759. Died young.
   3. Elizabeth Ann, baptized January 4, 1762. More further.

The promising career of Button Gwinnett ended tragically on May 19, 1777, when he died, at age 42, of wounds sustained three days earlier in a duel with General Lachlan McIntosh. Gwinnett's will, probated in Savannah, named another signer, Dr. Lyman Hall, as executor, who proceeded over many years to settle the estate of Gwinnett.

Mrs. Ann Gwinnett eventually moved to Charleston, South Carolina, where she was living on October 20, 1780 (while the British occupied the city), when she wrote a codicil to her will. She died sometime between then and May 4, 1785, when her will was probated. As with almost everything concerning her husband, her place of death and burial are unclear. A copy of her will and the probation of her estate were recorded by her son-in-law, Peter Belin, in the Prerogative Court of Canterbury, where estates of persons with land in both England and the colonies were recorded.

Elizabeth Ann Gwinnett (1762-c. 1785), youngest daughter of Button and Ann Gwinnett, married March 26, 1779, Peter Belin, (pronounced *Blaine*), of Huguenot descent, believed to be a son of Margaret (Robert) and Allard Belin (1719-1774), of Prince

George's Parish, South Carolina. She died without a will, but she may have been living in her grandmother's hometown of Brewood at the time of her death. Her husband administered her estate in February 1785, in the Prerogative Court of Canterbury.

As with her mother, her place of death and burial are unclear, as is the status of any children she had. There is some belief that she and Peter had issue, but that they died young. No one is known to have ever claimed descent from her.

Nothing is known of the date and circumstances of the death of Peter Belin. In 1779, he was on a jury list in Prince George's Parish, South Carolina, and he received land grants in South Carolina in 1786. In 1788, he was recorded in Georgia's Camden County as receiving a power-of-attorney. In 1789, he applied for a headright for himself and four slaves in Camden County. This appears to indicate that he had no wife or children at that time. In 1792, still in Camden County, he made articles of agreement with Robert Goodloe Harper (1765-1825) of Charleston (later a congressman), William Clay Snipes (1742-1806) of St. Bartholomew's Parish, South Carolina, and Mordecai Gist (1743-1792) of St. Andrew's Parish, South Carolina. After this time, all trace is lost.

On November 3, 1824, an advertisement appeared in the *Savannah Daily Georgian* from the Hope Insurance Office of New York City seeking information on the heirs of "Ann Gwinnett afterwards Beline."

Charles Francis Jenkins (1865-1951) of Philadelphia became an avid fan of Gwinnett and wrote the definitive biography, *Button Gwinnett: Signer of the Declaration of Independence* (1926), as well as a smaller booklet, *The Gwinnett Bible* (1926), and other writings. His papers are located at the Historical Society of Pennsylvania and the Georgia Department of Archives and History.

Arthur J. Funk (1898-1975) of Savannah spent many years collecting information on Gwinnett, and his biggest discovery was Gwinnett's grave in the Colonial Cemetery of Savannah.

This led to an excavation at the site in 1957, with a subsequent report issued by the Savannah-Chatham County Historic Site and Monument Commission, *The Burial Place of Button Gwinnett* (1959). Augusta tried to get the bones for the Signers' Monument in 1960; but Funk and Savannah won out, and the bones were reburied. An appropriate monument was dedicated on October 19, 1964, in Colonial Cemetery.

A portrait of Button Gwinnett by Jeremiah Theus, a prominent Charleston, South Carolina, artist, was discovered in 1958 and authenticated, amid the usual controversy that surrounds everything pertaining to the subject. The portrait is owned by Fulton Federal Savings and Loan Association, and is on display at its Pryor Street office in downtown Atlanta. Other items, including more of the rare Gwinnett signatures, have been discovered over the years. The 1927 sale of one of his letters for $51,000 is still considered the highest price ever paid for a single letter.

Gwinnett, a rare, if existent, surname in America, is still borne by some English families. Amid the Jenkins and Funk papers at the Georgia archives and the Georgia Historical Society are many letters from individuals attempting to establish collateral kinship with the signer. There were several Gwinnetts living in Wolverhampton in 1926, and in October 1975, Gwinnett County, Georgia, the only place in the state named for the signer, was visited by Andrew Gwinnett of Australia and England, yet another kinsman.

William Herbert Willson III (b. 1919), of Port Washington, South Pender Island, British Columbia, Canada, traces his descent from William Gwinnett (b.c. 1734), whom he believes to have been another brother of Button Gwinnett. Willson's grandmother was born Georgiana Gwinnett in Wolverhampton, where her brother William lived at "Winchelsea" in the 1920s.

GEORGE WALTON was born in 1749 or 1750 in Cumberland County, Virginia, and died February 2, 1804, "at his seat near

Augusta," Georgia. His funeral was held at his home, "Meadow Garden," and he was originally buried at the family cemetery at "Rosney," near Augusta. His remains, along with those of Lyman Hall, were reburied in Augusta under the Signers' Monument shortly before its cornerstone was laid July 4, 1848. "Meadow Garden," his home in Augusta, is owned and operated as a museum by the Georgia State Society, Daughters of the American Revolution. The house is on the National Register of Historic Places.

George Walton was the last son, and last child, of Robert Walton (b. c. 1717 and d. c. 1749/50 in Cumberland Co., Va.) and Mary Hughes, who had married c. 1740. He came to Georgia "at the age of 18," c. 1768, and settled in Savannah, where he became an attorney.

He married in September 1778, in Savannah, Dorothy Camber (b. c. 1763; d. September 12, 1832, in Pensacola, Florida where she is buried in St. Michael's Churchyard). Her house in Pensacola is on the National Register of Historic Places and is open as a museum. Dorothy Camber was one of the three daughters of Thomas Camber, a planter of Georgia and South Carolina, whose will was probated in Charleston in 1774.

Mrs. Walton's mother, Dorothy Butler (d. 1778), who became the second wife of Thomas Camber in 1762, was a daughter of Richard Butler (d.c. 1735 in S.C.) and his wife Sarah (d.c. 1756-1759). Richard owned land on the Ashley River that was later owned by another daughter, Mary, who married (3) Henry Hyrne. Mary's grandson John Drayton (1766-1822), who owned Drayton Hall near Charleston and was later governor of South Carolina (1800-1802), and Charles Cotesworth Pinckney (1745-1825), were her executors in 1795.

Another of Thomas Camber's daughters was Polly (a half-sister of Mrs. Walton), who married May 23, 1775, at Great Ogeechee, Georgia, Adam Fowler Brisbane (b. 1754, who died at his Richland District, S.C., plantation July 1, 1797); she died

SIGNERS' MONUMENT, AUGUSTA
The bodies of George Walton and Lyman Hall were reinterred here in 1848.

Augusta 19, 1820, in Camden, Kershaw District, South Carolina, age 65. The Brisbane descendants are traced in *The South Carolina Historical and Genealogical Magazine* (Vol. 14 (1913) pp. 187-97). The other daughter was Ann Sarah ("Nancy") Camber, b. c. 1765, who married March 19, 1783, probably in Savannah, Major John Habersham, of the Georgia Regiment and commandant of the town of Savannah. Major Habersham died, age 45, on November 19, 1799, and his wife died on March 9, 1802. Their descendants are traced in Joseph G.B. Bulloch's *History and Genealogy of the Habersham Family* (Columbia, S.C., 1901).

George and Dorothy Camber Walton had two sons:

1. Thomas Camber, born c. 1782. He was an attorney in Augusta and died, unmarried, at "Meadow Garden" on December 13, 1803.

2. George, Jr. (c. 1789-1863). More further.

George Walton, Jr. (b. c. 1789; d. Jan. 3, 1863, at Petersburg, Va. and is buried there in the city-owned Blenford Cemetery). An attorney, he was elected to the Georgia House of Representatives to serve Richmond County in the 1810-'11, 1816-'19 sessions. In 1821 he was appointed secretary of the territory of East Florida under Governor Andrew Jackson; and, when Jackson left, he completed the remainder of his term as acting governor. Walton was secretary for the combined territory of East-West Florida (1822-'26). Walton County, Florida, and Fort Walton Beach, Florida, are named for him. He left Pensacola around 1835 and moved to Mobile, Alabama, where he was mayor c. 1837-c. 1839. After a time, he and his wife parted, and he lived the remainder of his life in Washington, D.C., and Virginia.

He had married January 10, 1809 at "Bellevue," near Augusta, Sally Minge Walker, daughter of George Walker (d. Sept. 15, 1804, age 38, in Augusta), an attorney, and Eliza Talbot Walker (d. Nov. 21, 1842, age 66, in Augusta). The latter had married May 18, 1790, in Richmond County, Georgia.

George Walker was the first person to be buried in the Walker Cemetery, now located on the campus of Augusta College, formerly the Augusta Arsenal, and before that his estate "Bellevue."

Sally Minge Walker Walton was born in Washington, Georgia, on July 19, 1792, and died in Mobile, Alabama, on January 14, 1861, where she is buried in Magnolia Cemetery.

George and Sally Walker Walton had two children:

1. Octavia Celeste Valentine (1811-1877). More further.

2. Robert Watkins (b. 1812 in Augusta; d. Mar. 22, 1849, in Mobile, Ala.; buried in Magnolia Cemetery). He was admitted to the bar, helped organize the Mobile Rifle Co. in 1836 for the Creek Wars, and was a major in that unit when he died, unmarried.

Octavia C.V. Walton was born at "Bellevue," August 11, 1811, and died March 12, 1877, in Augusta, Georgia. She is buried in the Walker Cemetery.

Octavia became one of the most accomplished women of the 19th century, much of this being due to her early upbringing and travel. She moved with her parents in 1821 to Florida and learned to speak several languages. In 1833 she was presented to society in Washington, D.C., and in 1835 she moved to Mobile with her parents. Her mother had been grooming her for the "right" marriage, and in 1836 she married Dr. Henry S. LeVert, a physician. Throughout her brilliant social career she received various honors and compliments, among these being a poem in her name by Edgar Allen Poe; John C. Calhoun's referring to her as "the gifted daughter of the South"; and a long-standing friendship with Senator Henry Clay of Kentucky. A high point in her career came with her European tours of 1853 and 1855, which she related in her two-volume *Souvenirs of Travel* (1857).

While the Civil War ensued, Madame LeVert remained in Mobile and aided the Confederacy. The end of the war brought an end to the society to which she was accustomed, and she eventually closed her home in Mobile and returned to Augusta. Her home there, known as "Chateau LeVert," was razed in the early 1960s. It was there that she died in 1877.

Her husband, Dr. Henry S. LeVert, was born in King William County, Virginia, December 26, 1804, and died March 15, 1864, in Mobile, Alabama, having been in declining health for many years. He is buried there in Magnolia Cemetery.

According to Madame LeVert's diary, they had five children in the first ten years of marriage:

1. Octavia "Didi" Walton, born c. 1837 in Alabama; died in 1889 in Augusta. Unmarried.

2. Claudia Anna Eugenia, born c. 1837-'38; died May 8, 1849, age 11, of scarlet fever and buried in Magnolia Cemetery, Mobile, Alabama.

3. Sally Walker Walton, born c. 1840-'41; died May 3, 1849, age 8, of scarlet fever and buried in Magnolia Cemetery, Mobile.

4. Son who died at birth.

5. "Cara Netta" (born Henrietta Caroline and named for and by Henry Clay), born December 6, 1846. More further.

Cara Netta LeVert was born December 6, 1846, and died in Augusta, December 15, 1876; buried in the Walker Cemetery. She married, c. 1868, her cousin, Lawrence Augustus Regail Reab (b. December 16, 1844, d. July 3, 1909; buried in the Walker Cemetery). He was the son of George B. Reab and his first wife, Anna Euphemia Emma Re'Gail Walker, who were married in Augusta on November 23, 1839. Anna was the daughter of George M. Walker (b. in Va., c. 1789; d. Oct. 1, 1863, in Augusta; buried in Walker Cemetery) and Mary Tyler Walker (b. c. 1793 and d. in Augusta, Aug. 27, 1864, age 71). Mary T. Walker was a daughter of George and Eliza Talbot Walker (see foregoing).

George Brown Reab married (2) Charlotte N. Huger of Charleston (b. c. 1826 in England; d. in Augusta, Jan. 10, 1888, and buried in Walker Cemetery).

Cara Netta and Lawrence A. R. Reab had three children:

1. Regail LeVert, born August 31, 1870; died May 7, 1871. Buried in Walker Cemetery.

2. Infant, died young. Buried in Walker Cemetery.

3. George Walton was born June 17, 1873 (?) and died March 6, 1925, in Augusta, unmarried. Buried in the Walker Cemetery. At his death, just a year before the 150th aniversary of the Declaration of Independence, the direct line of descent from George Walton, the signer, ended. Reab had become the heir to much of his grandmother Madame LeVert's possessions, including her renowned scrapbook. Most of this was distributed, sold, or lost during his lifetime — a great loss to researchers.

Descendants in Augusta of the second marriage of Lawrence A. R. Reab, to Maria Jenkins (1859-1931), are: Margie Ann Rossignol (Mrs. Miller) Meyer; William A. Rossignol; Laura Reab (Mrs. Charles) Bowen (b. 1907); Anne Reab (Mrs. William M.) Berry (b. 1912); and Lawrence Reab Berry. Although not descended from the signer, they have many items of memorabilia that relate to the descendants of Madame LeVert.

Other Waltons in Georgia — There are many families in Georgia that descend from the sister or brothers of the signer or other relatives.

George Walton, uncle of the signer, is often confused in the public records with him. The uncle was born c. 1724 in Virginia and died there c. 1796. He married c. 1749 Martha Hughes (1734-1815), sister to the signer's mother. The uncle lived in Virginia but owned some land in Georgia. George and Martha Walton had a large family with many descendants in Georgia. One descendant was Lucian Lamar Knight (1868-1933), state historian of Georgia and director of the Georgia Department of Archives and History.

George Walton, the other, whose kinship is unknown, lived in Wilkes County, Georgia, and received land grants there in the 1780s. A George Walton, Jr., first cousin to the signer and a captain in the patriot forces, died in 1777 with no known descendants. A George Walton was appointed Georgia's commissar general in 1777, but it is unclear as to which one of these men it was.

John Walton, brother of the signer, was born 1743 and

married in 1769 in Augusta, Elizabeth Claiborne, daughter of Leonard Claiborne. They lived in Richmond County and had descendants, some of whom are listed hereafter.

Sally Walton, sister of the signer, born 1745, married (1) c. 1763 Thomas Watkins, Jr., of Powhatan, Virginia, who was killed in the Revolution and (2) Joshua Morris of Kentucky; children by both. Her descendants have included sons Robert and George Watkins, who edited the laws of Georgia in *Watkins Digest* (1800), which was the first such compilation of Georgia law; Miss Nell Harper; John C. Harper; J. Walker Harper, attorney; Ann Harper (Mrs. Thomas) Blanchard, all of Augusta; Mary Harper (Mrs. Andrew B.) Speed of Columbus Georgia; and Marie C. Robertson (Mrs. Albert Speiss of Opelousas, Louisiana. The last-named is currently researching this line.

The late R.C. Ballard Thruston (d. 1946) of Louisville, Kentucky, researched the Walton family in the 1920s, and his papers are with the Filson Club of Louisville. Miss Nell Harper of Augusta has much of his correspondence with her family.

Caldwell Delaney of the City of Mobile Museum Department is continuing research on Madame Octavia LeVert, who lived in that city for over thirty years.

Edwin C. Bridges of Atlanta wrote his dissertation in history for the University of Chicago entitled "George Walton: A Political Biography." The first definitive biography of the signer, it is the basis for the abbreviated version that appears in this volume.

Mary W. Meadows has compiled *From Virginia, New England, Saint Dominique, West Indies . . . the Genealogy of the Families Formon-Boisclair, Walker, Beers, Lacy* (1980), which includes the Walker and Walton families of Augusta.

(This sketch is based on an article that appeared in *Georgia Life* in the Spring of 1976. It is reprinted with the permission of the publisher.)

Credit for Illustrations

The authors acknowledge their indebtedness and their appreciation to the following sources for the illustrations indicated:

"The Declaration of Independence," by John Trumbull, a mural in the United States Capitol — Library of Congress.

Georgia's Revolutionary Flags — Office of the Secretary of the State of Georgia.

Liberty Boys, Crowd of Whig Sympathizers — Artist's sketches from *Stories of Georgia*, by Joel Chandler Harris, published in Atlanta: Cherokee Publishing Company, 1971 (reprint of the original, published in New York: 1896).

View of Savannah, by Joseph Louis Firmin Cerveau — Georgia Historical Society.

Portrait of Lyman Hall — Special Collections, University of Georgia Libraries, Athens, Georgia.

Map of Colonial Georgia — Research by Marion R. Hemperly; cartography by Jerri H. Hager.

Portrait of Button Gwinnett, by Jeremiah Theus — Fulton Federal Savings and Loan Association, Atlanta, Georgia.

Drawing of Gwinnett-McIntosh Duel — from *Button Gwinnett, Signer of the Declaration of Independence*, by Charles F. Jenkins, published in New York: Doubleday, Doran & Company, 1926.

Photograph of Grave of Button Gwinnett — Georgia Historical Society, Savannah, Georgia.

Portrait of George Walton, by Charles Wilson Peale — Yale University Art Gallery (Mabel Brady Garvan Collection).

Portrait of Georgia's Signers of the Declaration of Independence Atlanta Historical Society (Trust Company of Georgia Collection).

Photoghaph of "Meadow Garden," Home of George Walton — Georgia Society, Daughters of the American Revolution; from the papers of Ms. Harriet Grubb Jeffries.

Photograph of Signers' Monument, Augusta, Georgia — State Department of Archives & History, Atlanta, Georgia.

Cover illustration: Portrait of Georgia's Signers of the Declaration of Independence — Atlanta Historical Society.

The Authors

Edwin C. Bridges is assistant director for administrative services at the Georgia Department of Archives and History. He grew up in Bainbridge, Georgia, attended Furman University, and received his Ph.D. from the University of Chicago, where he wrote his dissertation on George Walton. He has also taught history in high school and college and has worked as a historical research consultant for the Historic Preservation Section of the Georgia Department of Natural Resources.

Harvey H. Jackson is associate professor of history and chairman of the Division of Social Sciences at Clayton Junior College. He is the author of *Lachlan McIntosh and the Politics of Revolutionary Georgia,* and his articles have appeared in the *William and Mary Quarterly, Georgia Historical Quarterly, Atlanta Historical Journal, American History Illustrated, Georgia Gazette, Register of the Kentucky Historical Society,* and *Southern Studies.*

Kenneth H. Thomas, Jr., is a historian for the Historic Preservation Section of the Georgia Department of Natural Resources; in that capacity he has written a series of published research reports on historic sites in Georgia. He has also written a quarterly column, "Georgia Family Lines," for *Georgia Life,* and currently writes a weekly column on genealogy for the Sunday *Atlanta Journal-Constitution*. He is on the board of editors of the *Dictionary of Georgia Biography* and has coordinated the compilation of a directory for the Georgia Association of Museums and Galleries.

James Harvey Young is Charles Howard Candler Professor of American Social History at Emory University, where he has taught for forty years. In addition, he is the president of the Southern Historical Association for 1981. He has published in the field of American medical history and the history of food and drug regulation. His interest in Lyman Hall sprang from the fact that Hall was one of the handful of physicians to sign the Declaration. Professor Young is the author of *The Toadstool Millionaires*, *The Medical Messiahs*, and *American Self-Dosage Medicine*.

Index

Printed in the United States
29802LVS00006B/243

9 780877 973157